Jewish Culture. A Quick Immersion

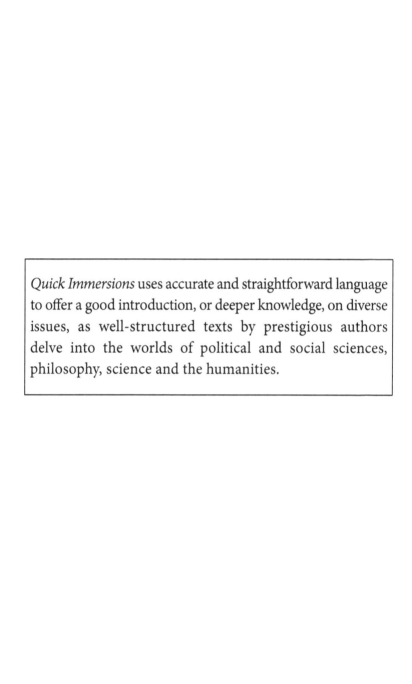

Quick Immersions uses accurate and straightforward language to offer a good introduction, or deeper knowledge, on diverse issues, as well-structured texts by prestigious authors delve into the worlds of political and social sciences, philosophy, science and the humanities.

Jess Olson

JEWISH CULTURE
A Quick Immersion

Tibidabo Publishing

Copyediting by Lori Gerson
Cover art by Raimon Guirado
For illustration copyrights, please see page 7.

First published 2019

Visit our Series on our Web:
www.quickimmersions.com

ISBN: 978-1-949845-10-5
1 2 3 4 5 6 7 8 9 10

Printed in the United States of America.

Contents

List of illustrations copyrights

Introduction:
What is Jewish Culture?

What is Jewish culture? This may seem like a question
with a straightforward answer: it is the culture of the
collective Jewish people. And who are they? Again,
straightforward: they are those who identify with
the religion of Judaism, an ancient monotheistic
faith that has grown and survived for millennia, and
despite its tiny share of the world population, was
the direct ancestor of both the major monotheistic
religions today, Christianity and Islam. Or perhaps
Jews are part of an ethnic group that coalesced
around a shared history as a religious group, but
whose real links are familial and genetic? Or perhaps
they are a national group that has existed since
antiquity, has somehow failed to disintegrate after
its national center collapsed, only to create a new
version in the modern state of Israel? Or is it none of
these, but rather a construct, a set of identifications
with ideas about history, religion, and humanity
that at various times and various places has taken
different, evolving forms?

So the question is not so simple after all. In fact, Jews can be fairly described through all of these lenses. Many Jews do practice the Jewish religion in some form, and from the perspective of many of its devotees today, especially those who describe themselves as "Orthodox" (more on this below), belief in the divinity of the Torah, the central text of Judaism, and its laws is the essence of Judaism.

Yet many more Jews reject this definition of identity. Most Jews in the world today are not Orthodox, and many would not define themselves in terms of religious belief at all. Conversely, it is an essential belief within Orthodoxy that a person be considered Jewish according to guidelines that, though grounded in religious precepts, are clearly derived from an ethnic idea of Jewishness. Unlike Islam and many branches of Christianity with a doctrinal idea of religious identity, a person not born to a Jewish mother (or, in some liberal expressions of Judaism, a Jewish parent) or who does not undergo a legalistic process of conversion to Judaism is not considered a Jew simply through profession of belief.

So perhaps Jews are some form of genetically related group, like a family or ethnicity? Again, this is also a persuasive position, and one that likely resonates with far more Jewish individuals. For centuries, the Diaspora (the community of Jews who live outside the land of Israel) defined the experience of most Jews in the world. In every society in which they have lived in the Diaspora, Jews were a minority group. Due to a combination of inner-group taboo and external prejudice over most of this 2,000 year history, Jews were unusually endogamous (married within the group). Within the Jewish community, it was historically unacceptable, and remains so to some, to marry outside the faith, and until the nineteenth century marriage outside the community was exceedingly rare. From the position of the two dominant societies amongst whom Jews lived for most of this period—Islamic North Africa, Levant, and Middle East, and Christian Europe and the Americas—Jews were a tolerated but frequently despised group, culturally and socially isolated. Marriage with Jews was rare and usually demanded the conversion of the Jewish person out of the religion.

But this option of conversion calls into question the durability of the ethnic category. Movement between faiths—both out of Judaism and into Christianity or Islam and vice-versa—has been a consistent feature of interfaith interactions over history. And while, in some instances, conversion out of Judaism was suspect and viewed as inadequate to "change" the identity of the convert, this was unusual until the nineteenth century and the advent of pseudo-biological racism. Similarly, conversion to Judaism, while not a common practice (although it has become more common in the last half-century than possibly any time in Diaspora Jewish history) has always existed as an option within rabbinic

Judaism. Numerous "righteous converts," as individuals who convert to Judaism out of religious conviction are called, have played important roles in the evolution of Jewish history and religious thought. Jewish law, or halakha, considers full acceptance of a genuine convert to Judaism as a Jewish person in all respects a solemn obligation. In addition, explicit indications in the central texts of Judaism show that the intense endogamy and taboo against marriage with outsiders was not so clear-cut before the dispersion of ancient Israel in the first century CE.

How about Jews as a national group? Similar to ethnicity, this definition would seem to have potential. After all, as is also explicit in the Bible, Israel as an ancient nation (which should not be conflated with the modern idea of the nation) was essential to the classical conception of Judaism. According to these texts, the Israelites descended into Egypt in the time of the Pharaohs as an extended family. While in Egypt, the experience of bitter enslavement kept the ancient Hebrews connected as a clan-based social class in Egyptian society that was considered distinct from the surrounding culture. In classical rabbinic terms, the Jews of Egypt, although in all other ways disconnected from the faith of their ancestor Abraham, retained their unique names, clothing and language—which may be understood as stand-ins for national markers of identity. After the exodus, the central moment of nation-formation in Israelite history, the Israelites were given a legal code (the Torah), a structure of basic governance, and a group identity around a particularist deity whose instructions sought to mold the people into a conquering nation over forty years in the desert. This process culminated in an actual invasion of the "Land of Canaan" and the displacement of other, idolatrous peoples that dwelt there. Even to modern eyes, this process resembles a national mission and conquest.

Israelite sovereignty was ultimately destroyed, along with the Beit Hamikdash (Temple), its center of worship, by legions of the Roman Empire in the first century CE. Although it took nearly two thousand years, a construct of the Jewish nation, this time in modern form, was ultimately created once again, in the Jewish nation-state of Israel. To many theorists of modern Zionism, this was precisely the basis of Jewish identity. Some of the most important early theorists of Zionism such as essayist Ahad Ha'am (Asher Ginsberg), nationalism was the core identity, both genetically and spiritually, of all peoples, including the Jews. While the Diaspora had demanded sublimation of this identity into religion, which served as a preservative for Jewish peoplehood in its long exile, they believed it was national identity that represented the true essence of Judaism.

Picture 1. Emblem of the State of Israel, which incorporates symbols of ancient Israel, in particular the Menorah, one of the vessels of the ancient Temple.

Yet this identity was, and remains, explicitly rejected by a considerable number of Jews, for several reasons. Although the State of Israel's establishment in 1948 consolidated much of world Jewish opinion in support of the new state, many in the Orthodox community had long rejected, and indeed actively struggled against, the growth of secular Zionism and its ambitions in the land of Israel before 1948. This attitude changed dramatically after the creation of the state, and especially after what many considered a miraculous deliverance in the 1967 war. At the same time, ambivalence and even hostility to the secular state is still widespread in the Haredi (conservative Orthodox) community. Likewise, a great number of Jews of other denominations, and those who do not practice Judaism in any religious form, bristle at Israeli demands for loyalty from Jews in the Diaspora as a core identity. In its most critical form, some Jews in the Diaspora view it as presumptuous that Israel, an independent state with its own policy and culture, should demand their support through an appeal to Jewish identity. Although positive identification with Israel in the Diaspora is far more prevalent among Jews than opposition to it, as in the Orthodox world, sympathy does not come without a measure of ambivalence. After all, most Diaspora Jews consider themselves citizens of their own country, not citizens of a Jewish nation state.

Or perhaps it is none of these. For many Jews, particularly in the United States, Judaism is a combination of ethnic identity (which may or may not coincide with the religious definition), a sense of self, an identification with aspects of the Jewish experience, even simply marriage to a Jewish spouse. For many American Jews, Judaism represents the tolerance and humanity that they see in the best aspects of the American ideal. Indeed, especially after a massive influx of impoverished Russian Jews emerged as the backbone of American Judaism in the early twentieth century, their identity as Jews became a prism through which they saw many external engagements, from politics, to education, to social class. For many, the idea of the family, the household, and the community became the essential basis of their Jewish identity, whether or not they had any formal affiliation with what would be understood as either its religious or its national institutions. For a considerable number of Jews in the United States today, being Jewish simply does not have a straightforward set of defining characteristics.

We are left with our questions: what are Jews, and what is Jewish culture?

Brief History of Jewish Demographics and Places of Residence

To begin answering these questions, it is useful to gain a clearer picture of this population. In the world today, according to the most reliable estimates, there are approximately 14.6 million Jews. In only two countries, the United States and Israel, do Jews number more than one million. The population of Jews in the United States in 2018 was around 5.7 million. This number is probably a conservative estimate, as many who consider themselves Jewish in the United States are regularly excluded from surveys of the Jewish population, as the primary means of calculating the Jewish population in the US have been derived from counting those who participate in Jewish institutions, which many American Jews eschew. Israel's Jewish population is of the same magnitude, about 6.1 million. These numbers are not exact, and only recently has Israel's Jewish population come to slightly outnumber that of the United States. In any case, between them the United States and Israel count for over nine tenths of the entire population of Jews in the world. The next-largest Jewish population in any single country is France, which has fewer than 500,000 Jews, a population that is in decline; only a few other countries have more than 100,000 Jewish citizens.

This is a recent distribution of the Jewish world population in the long arc of Jewish history. As late as the 1930s, before the onset of the Second World War, the number of Jews worldwide was nearly the same to what it is in 2019, around 14 million. The largest population of about 9.5 million Jews then resided in Europe. The overwhelming majority of those Jews lived in east-central Europe, the largest numbers divided between Poland and the Soviet Union, with around 3 million and 2.5 million Jews, respectively. The United States at the time had around 4 million Jews, and in British Mandate Palestine, the territory of which part would become the State of Israel in 1948, there were less than 250,000. These numbers are consistent in terms of demographic distribution for much of modern history, with the exception of Mandate Palestine and the United States. These regions saw a considerable growth in their Jewish populations between 1881 and the

1920s due to intensified migration to escape poverty and persecution in Russia and Poland. While Jews lived in other regions, primarily in North Africa, southeastern Europe, Anatolia and the Levant, and further east as far as Iran, these communities were far smaller; the total number of Jews in these countries was under one million before the creation of the State of Israel. Today, there are virtually no Jewish communities left in the Islamic world, and those in the former demographic centers of eastern Europe have almost entirely disappeared.

Diversity of Jewish Cultures in the Present Day

Given these numbers, what do Jewish communities look like today? What are their defining characteristics?

Jewish population of the United States

The Jewish population of the United States is as old as European settlement in the Americas, but the majority are descendants of later arrivals. The first significant wave was composed of German Jews in the mid-nineteenth century, the second, exponentially larger, were Jews fleeing late nineteenth and early twentieth-century tumult in the

Russian Empire. This included a massive influx of refugees between 1881 and the mid-1920s. To these numbers were added the refugees fleeing the spread of Nazism, and the even larger number of survivors fleeing postwar Europe after its vanquishment. It also includes smaller but still impactful waves of immigrants from the 1950s on from the Islamic world, the former Soviet Union and its client states, and even a number of Israeli ex-patriots in the last few decades.

American Jews are often characterized and define themselves by their level of religious observance in general assessments of the community's character. There is no centralized authority akin to a chief rabbinate or even a national umbrella organization representing Jews in the United States. Instead, several private bodies represent a spectrum of different formal expressions of Judaism. This model as a way of generalizing about American Jews is of decreasing value as more individuals, especially outside the Orthodox community, are not members of synagogues and seek meaning in their Jewish identity in other ways. It reflects a mid-twentieth century assumption that most Jews affiliate with a formal expression of religious practice. Nevertheless, there are three religious identities by which American Jews define themselves overwhelmingly: Orthodox, Reform and Conservative.

Two of these, Reform and Conservative, are the formal names of modern, liberal expressions of Judaism that evolved in the United States out of the intra-Jewish communal conflict in Germany in the first half of the nineteenth century. Between them, they claim the majority of American Jews who affiliate formally with Judaism through synagogue membership, but for decades these numbers have been declining. Members of these movements, having arisen originally out of an effort to modernize Jewish practice, are for the most part entirely integrated into American society, tend not to observe punctiliously (or at all) practices dictated by Jewish law. They tend to identify with their religious practice in much the same way that American Christians in liberal denominations of Christianity do: as part of their civic identity and a place for community, less because of a sense of doctrinal obligation. Participants in these versions of Judaism tend not to wear any overt markers of their identity, although some may wear a kippah (or yarmulke, a skullcap) as a statement of cultural solidarity or religious devotion.

The third group, the Orthodox, which usually numbers between twelve to fifteen percent of the overall American Jewish community, regards observance of Jewish law as an absolute obligation. At the same time, there is considerable diversity within the Orthodox community. At one end are those described as "modern" Orthodox, meaning that they maintain Orthodox religious practice but do not regard limited engagement with American culture as a threat to their identity. American modern Orthodox Jews speak English as their primary language, dress in modern clothing, and generally identify with the values of other middle and upper-middle class Americans, as well as sharing the same levels of affluence. Nevertheless, most modern Orthodox Jews do tend to wear visible markers of their identity: men will wear a kippah (skullcap) and often visible ritual fringes (tzitzit, which we will discuss in Chapter 1), and women will wear clothing in accordance with Jewish legal standards of modesty, as defined by their community (usually married women will cover their hair and will wear only skirts rather than trousers).

At the other extreme are more rejectionist Orthodox groups. The most familiar and visible are Hasidim, members of a specific form of Orthodox practice which rejects all but the minimal interaction with American culture required for economic stability. These groups are intensively insular, live in tight-knit and increasingly isolated communities (having largely shifted from their original centers in inner-city New York to its rural suburbs). Both men and women wear distinctive dress as obligatory expressions of their separation from non-Jews (and other Jews), and many groups speak Yiddish rather than English in their communities. Men, for the most part, wear black outer clothing, with the type of jacket varying depending on the group, white shirt, and a black hat—again, the style depending on the group. Women in these communities wear very conservative clothing, always skirts below the knee, thick stockings, sleeves which go below the elbow, and cover all of their own hair with a hat or wig (called a shaytl). Between these two extremes, there are many combinations and permutations of these cultural tendencies.

In the Diaspora outside of the United States, which includes communities on every continent, there are a few shared characteristics. First, as we have seen, these are small communities, but are often focused in large cities, such as Paris, Nice, Manchester, and London. Jews in these communities tend to be affiliated with a formal communal authority, and in places like the United Kingdom and France, there is a formal Jewish community with a recognized, centralized rabbinate and administration. Jews in these countries follow similar patterns of occupation, social class and cultural identification with Jews in the United States. That is to say, they tend to be middle and upper-middle class, tend towards white collar occupations and professions, and tend to dress similarly, speak the same language, and have similar cultural identification as their non-Jewish compatriots. One exception to this general similarity is that, in these smaller communities, Orthodox oversight of the communal institutions and membership in the community is standard, and the overall proportion of members who identify as Orthodox is significantly higher than in the United

States. This is a contentious point however, for in many of these communities there is no alternative in terms of places of worship or communal attachment save the official community, so many may not identify with strict Orthodox observance privately.

The Jewish Population of Israel

The Jewish population of the State of Israel, while sharing similarities with the Diaspora population, is also quite distinct. Unlike the United States, identity as a construct of a Jewish religious movement is almost irrelevant in Israeli society. Because being an Israeli perforce commits one to a national model of Jewish identity (even if it isn't accepted unambiguously, as in the Haredi community), those who do not identify with Judaism religiously tend not to have need for Jewish identity outside their secular citizenship. Many feel no need for membership in a religious organization to maintain a robust Jewish identity. The language of most Jews in Israel is Hebrew, a modern iteration of the language of the Jewish people since antiquity, and the central symbols of the state and Israeli society are derived from a construction of Zionist identity at the turn of the twentieth century.

For Israelis who do identify religiously, Orthodoxy tends to be the favored expression. While a small minority of non-Orthodox, religiously-active

Israeli Jews have worked to create a larger presence of Jewish religious diversity in Israel, they have been consistently frustrated, and it has been difficult to establish a sizable presence. An important reason for this is the centralized chief rabbinate, which is a government body that, since the state's inception, has been exclusively Orthodox, and thus hostile to liberal expressions of Judaism on principle (we will discuss this further in Chapter 3).

At the same time, there is an increasingly robust presence of Israel's version of the modern Orthodox, the dati leumi (national religious) in all arenas of life, including the military and government at the highest levels. The dati leumi tend to be intensely patriotic, and their interpretation of Zionism understands it as an outgrowth of their Orthodox belief. While diversity of opinions exist, they are important among the vanguard of supporters of hawkish military policy, expansive settlement in disputed areas, and conservative social and cultural policy. At the other extreme are the Haredim (term literally means "those who tremble" [before God]) which are the analog – and in some cases, identical with – more extreme conservative Orthodox groups in the United States. As elsewhere, they are insular and strive to isolate themselves culturally and physically from modern Israeli culture. They often speak Yiddish in their communities (some even view speaking modern Hebrew as a profanation of the sacred language). At the same time, the Haredim are a considerable social and cultural force in Israeli society. Although ambivalent about the Zionist identity of the state, they accept citizenship and, importantly, vote in large blocks to defend the prerogatives of the community and to fund their own institutions and culture. Unlike the dati leumi, they formally reject some important obligations of Israeli citizenship, especially military service or public service for the state. At the same time, like other groups, the Haredi community has a great deal of diversity, and increasingly many have found ways within their religious conviction to become more active and involved in Israeli society and culture. Indeed, today it is fairly common to encounter members of the Haredi community in nearly every walk of life in Israel.

While these descriptions are by necessity general and succinct, they will serve us well as we begin our "quick immersion" in the history and evolution of Jewish culture.

This Book and its Approach

In the end, then, what is Jewish identity, the basis of Jewish culture? Is it based in religion? Is it an ethnic identity? Is it a national identity?

In fact the best way to describe Jewish culture is that it contains all of these at once. Every Jewish individual, family and community negotiates some combination of these three identities. An Israeli

Orthodox Jew may simultaneously see themselves as defined by a collection of religious texts and rituals, and at the same time view them as inseparable from their citizenship of the State of Israel. It is almost certain that this person would view themselves as part of a "people," that is, an ethnic group, and they may well place high value on voting for their Knesset member (the parliamentary body of the State of Israel) based on their religious convictions—or not. A Jewish person in New York might not attend synagogue, speak or read Hebrew, observe only Passover and Yom Kippur with their families as a way of staying connected to Judaism, and who, when married, opts to raise their children "as Jews," meaning replicating their own identity even if they marry a non-Jewish partner. This person might see their identity as primarily ethnic, one of the many flavors of American diversity, but feel intrinsically that this identity makes them no less American. They may be a strong supporter of Israel, or they may be a critic of Israeli policy—in either case, their identity is in some way related to a national one, but clearly not in the same way as a citizen of Israel. The permutations of these identities are many.

Thus in this book, we will approach understanding Jewish culture through each of three primary "modes" of identity: religion, family and community, and nation. I will describe each of these as a different form of Jewish culture, but this is really an artificial distinction. Almost no Jewish person sees themselves exclusively through one form of identity only. In fact, each of these stories are in some sense the same story told through a different prism.

One benefit of this construction is that the book need not be read in linear order. Rather, depending on the approach and interests of the reader, it may be more illuminating to read in an order different than presented here. The order of presentation—religion, family and community, and nation—is arbitrary to a degree, and reflects a general sentiment that places religious belief and history at the center of Jewish culture. This is defensible, but hardly a necessary posture to take in a book such as this; nevertheless, it does not imply that one form of identity is or should be regarded as more important or central than the other two. All three of these, in my view, are vibrant, sometimes conflicting components of the inner and communal experience of most Jews. The reader will find that although each of these three stories resonates strongly with the other two, they are not at all identical, but complimentary.

This book is not a linear history, nor an exhaustive academic description of Jewish culture, but rather a collage of descriptions presented from the perspective of an informed insider to this culture. As an academic Jewish historian, trained in the methodologies of modern historical research and writing, who teaches at Yeshiva University in New York City, an American university with affiliation to the modern Orthodox community worldwide, and finally as a practicing Orthodox Jew, my identity is located at its own unique nexus of the various identities we will describe here. The impact of this on this text is both obvious and subtle: there is a clear orientation here towards building a deep, historical context to understand the various strains of Jewish culture. At the same time, I have selected carefully from the immense body of historical, religious, textual, philosophical, anthropological, sociological and other knowledge to present what I regard as giving the most vivid image of this world. I take the position of one on the boundaries between this world and the wider world. Thus, this book is written from the perspective of an informed insider trained to communicate, hopefully in a clear and agreeable way, the complexities of a culture and society that may often seem daunting or confusing to those who have never encountered them before.

Lastly, I have tried to present this portrait in language that accomplishes both a clear understanding but also, to the extent possible, an immersive experience. To this end, there is one peculiarity that the reader will notice immediately that may seem somewhat jarring: the use of Hebrew terms and their English translations. Throughout the text, when it is necessary to use a Hebrew word, I will provide the Hebrew in the text itself (in transliteration), and the English translation in parenthesis immediately after. After the first usage, I then utilize the Hebrew term more or less exclusively. I hope that this editorial decision will accomplish an impressionistic goal. Judaism is, in many ways, a language unto itself; the more that one speaks the language, the more one is able to make sense of the culture. While it is impossible in a book such as this (or even ten such books) to immerse a reader truly in the experience of Jewishness, I believe that a basic familiarity with the terms that Jews use themselves to describe their culture are essential in beginning to understand it.

With that, let us begin our quick immersion in Jewish culture.

Chapter 1
The Culture of Judaism: Religious Culture

Sacred Texts, Sacred History

The Jewish religion, one of the earliest forms of ethical monotheism, a religion that maintains the sole provenance of human morality and purpose is a unitary God, is also most commonly understood as the essence of Jewish identity. It remains a core identity for many Jews to this day. There is no consensus regarding the origins of the Jewish religion or the Jewish people, although there has been no lack of effort to discover them. Many speculate how such a belief system emerged, one so significantly different from most other forms of ancient religion. Explanations, mostly academic, range from the naturalistic (attempts to explain Biblical events through natural phenomena), to the historical (use of archeological and historical analysis of the text in tandem with external sources to verify events or personalities), to the literary (reading these texts as products of ancient literary culture utilizing identifiable devices and practices), to the psychological (seeking the origins of these religious texts as expressions of a universal component of the human psyche). In the end, each method has its value, but none capture the view of those who practice Judaism themselves, which is what we will explore in this chapter.

Ancient Origins

The origin of Judaism according to its own texts and traditions is straightforward. The ancient form of Judaism emerged from the spiritual awakening of a wanderer from Ur Kasdim (or Ur of the Chaldees, present-day southern Iraq), Abram, who is renamed Abraham at the initiation of his divine mission. The Bible's story of Abraham's origins is terse, describing the barest details of his genealogy, birthplace, and wife, Sarah. But no matter. His story sums up the core elements of Judaism in one passage: "And the Lord said to Abraham: 'Go forth from your native land and from your father's house to the land I will show you, I will make of you a great nation, and I will bless you; I will make your name great and you shall be a blessing, I will bless those that bless you, and curse him that curses you, and all the families of the Earth shall bless themselves by you.'"

"Go Forth from your Native Land…"

The foundational premises of ancient Judaism, the Israelite religion, are explicit in this brief passage. The first is the God that speaks to Abraham. Unique among other contemporary ancient religions, the idea of Judaism is identical with that of monotheism, of a single, disembodied and all-powerful God. Second is the act of God's communication with Abraham, that is, prophecy: linguistic and sensory communication from an abstract, formless Godhead to humanity to effect a moral directive in human society. The basis of Judaism is a formal agreement, a brit (covenant), literally understood to have been enacted between God and Abraham.

This is repeated frequently in the unfolding of the Bible's narrative, first with the directives of God to Abraham, his wife, his son Isaac and Isaac's wife Rebecca, his grandson Jacob and his wives Leah and Rachel, and finally his great-grandson Joseph. It culminates with the arrival and prophecy of Moses, to whom God presented the corpus of Jewish law and early history as inscribed in the Torah. The idea of God as the foundation of ethics and morality is essential, as is the idea of God as a figure whose will is enacted through those to whom he reveals himself, to whom he is partial and whose descendants, the Jewish people, are charged with the unique mission of carrying these ethical ideas and witnessing them before the rest of humanity.

Third, Judaism is understood by its adherents as rooted in the land "that I will show you." This is the destination of Abraham's long wanderings, the mountainous region about seventy kilometers from the mid-coast of the eastern Mediterranean, the central region of what is now the cities of Jerusalem, Hebron and Jericho (expanded in the Torah during the return of the Hebrews from Egyptian exile to include all of present-day Israel, the West Bank, and a significant section of present-day Jordan).

The importance of the written text in the emergence of this tradition was profound and has always remained a central element of Jewish identity, regardless of period or culture, whether in times of Jewish sovereignty or exile. The appellation "People of the Book," a common reference term for the Jewish people preserved both inside and outside the Jewish world, attests to the centrality of text in the history of the Jewish religion. The foundational text of Judaism, the Torah, maintained to this day in its ancient form as a scroll, remains the central ritual object of Judaism, regardless of its denomination or expression.

The Torah and Tanakh

Composed of five different "books," (sefarim in Hebrew), the Torah is traditionally believed to have been given directly to Moses by God after he had led the Jewish people out of slavery in Egypt. In Orthodox circles, this belief is an unshakable conviction and solemn matter of faith, the first link in a chain of unadulterated transmission of Jewish tradition from the giving of the Torah to Moses up to this day. The plain text of the Torah is understood to contain the totality of possible interpretations as guidelines for human behavior and ethics, down to the finest details of daily life. It is likewise understood in traditional circles to contain the boundaries of allowable interpretation, as well as those who are qualified to interpret and establish the meaning of the text. This authority initially lay with Moses himself in concert with his brother, Aaron, who became the patriarch of the priestly caste. The Torah records Moses' expansion of this interpretive authority to an early form of a religious "court" of sorts—the rudiments of Israelite governance.

At various points in the Torah, Moses is shown using a combination of direct revelation and textual exegesis (interpretation and explanation) to provide guidance in interpreting the Torah as necessary during the Israelites' wandering in the desert. After Moses' death, this process continued. The text depicts Joshua, Moses' successor as leader of the

Israelites, as continuing to receive direct instruction from God as well as to further the definition and refinement of exegetical principles. According to rabbinic Judaism, the ancestor of contemporary Judaism, while God continued to communicate directly with individual humans (the Prophets, or Nevi'im, as well as certain key historical leaders, namely the kings Saul, David and Solomon), these communications did not create new understandings or interpretations of the Torah itself, but rather exhortations to the Jewish people to atone when they strayed from its precepts. Over time, the Jewish tradition ended the legitimacy of divine revelation entirely as a valid tool of interpretation, and a relatively new scholarly class rose in significance, the ancient rabbinate.

Picture 2. Man reading from a Torah scroll

Among non-Orthodox Jews, there are various attitudes towards the integrity of this tradition and the belief in the direct revelation of the Torah to Moses. Attitudes range from acceptance of *part* of the idea of divine revelation of the Torah—for example, that the *written* Torah (that is, the five books of Moses' Pentateuch) were given by God, and the elaboration of the laws into codes of conduct of human behavior evolved through human interpretation. Another view, shared widely by those who subscribe to the Reform movement, is that all of the sacred texts of Judaism are of human origin, compiled by multiple authors over the eons, but which together present a vision of divine intention for human behavior and ethics. Especially important in this conception of Judaism is the model of ethical monotheism and the historical mission of the Jewish people to convey this ideal to the non-Jewish world. Still others, many of whom identify in some way with Judaism as a religious belief, deny any divinity to the texts and view them as important works of ancient literature, yet adhere to aspects of religion for reasons of identity or family, among others.

The Hebrew Bible, of which the Torah is a part, is composed of three collections of texts, referred to together as the Tanakh, a Hebrew acronym derived from the first letters of each section: "Ta" (for Torah), "Na" (for "Nevi'im," prophets), and Kh (for "Ketuvim" or homiletic and literary writings). The opening "book" of the Torah, Bereshit (Genesis) tells the Jewish version of creation and the early history of humanity up to the calling of Abraham to adopt the God of the Bible as the exclusive God. It then follows the trajectory of Abraham's son, Isaac, and Isaac's son, Jacob, and his twelve sons, most importantly his second-youngest son, Joseph, who is sold by his brothers to slavery in Egypt. Joseph's genius and prophetic insight enables him to rise to a high rank in Pharaoh's court, and leads to the subsequent migration of Jacob's family to Egypt.

The remaining bulk of the Torah is made up of the books Shemot (Exodus), Vayikra (Leviticus), Bamidbar (Numbers), and Devarim (Deuteronomy). These tell the story of the birth, encounter with God, and rebellion against the Egyptians of the figure Moses. Under God's command and protection, Moses leads the enslaved descendants of Jacob out of Egyptian bondage in a miraculous process of redemption. After the Exodus, the Torah describes the revelation of the Torah to Moses, the process of adopting and incorporating the formidable code of human behavior (the *mitzvot*, or "commandments," which touch upon nearly every aspect of individual, family and communal life), and the other events that galvanized the ancient Israelite people into a religious, social and political collective. Mostly the Torah is a digest of the obligations that Jews understand tie them to God and represent God's authoritative revelation to humanity. At the same time, these sections of the Torah describe the process of preparation for the culminating promise signified by God's election of the Jewish people for revelation of the Torah: their return to the land promised to Abraham as the reward for his obedience to God's call, the Land of Israel (also referred to in the texts as the "Land of Canaan").

The collection of texts grouped in the Hebrew Bible under the name "Nevi'im," or "Prophets," continues the Torah's historical narrative following the death of Moses, who was tragically denied the merit of entering into the reclaimed land. It begins with the details of Joshua's miraculous reconquest of the land by the descendants of the original exiles from Egypt as the Israelites establish their first political entity. Successive texts describe the evolving political structure of the first Israelite commonwealth through a series of tribal and charismatic leaders (the "Judges," or Shoftim), and finally the emergence of a dynastic monarchy —beginning unsuccessfully with Saul, and then a golden era under David and his son, Solomon. During this period, the religious ideal of the Jewish state, with its cultic center in a Temple atop the sacred mountain (known colloquially in Hebrew as "Har Habayit," "the mountain of the Home," that is, the dwelling place of God), which is traditionally identified with the location of God's revelation of the divine covenant to Abraham.

Nevi'im also contains a collection of the central, post-Torah era prophetic texts, which date chronologically from the end of the reigns of David and Solomon to the conquest of the Israelite state by the Babylonian king Nebuchadnezzar, and the seventy years of the first exile of the Jewish people in Babylon. Noted for their poetic beauty (such as Eliyahu/Elijah) and often outlandish aesthetic and striking description of supernatural visions (such as found in Yehezkel/Ezekiel), the prophetic books are widely appreciated for the power and inspiration of their ethical admonishment in the years leading up to, and during, the Babylonian exile.

The final section of the Tanakh, "Ketuvim," or "writings" includes collections of devotional poetry (such as Tehillim, the Psalms, traditionally attributed to King David) and ethical instruction (Mishlei, or Proverbs, attributed to Solomon). It contains further elaborations of Jewish history, most importantly the return of a portion of the exiled Jewish people back to Jerusalem and its surrounding areas, the creation of a quasi-autonomous Jewish protectorate under the Persian monarch Cyrus the Great, and the reconstruction of the Temple and the resumption of national worship on the Temple Mount. Finally, Ketuvim is the home of the five megillot (scrolls), which include five texts that are part of the liturgy for the major holidays of the Jewish calendar: Esther, Shir Hashirim (Song of Songs), Eichah (Lamentations), Ruth, and Kohelet (Ecclesiastes). Some of these texts (Esther and Ruth) recount historical vignettes with a devotional theme relevant to the holiday upon which the texts are read out loud to the community. The others are mostly poetic meditations on holiday-related themes.

Development of Jewish Legal Literature

A central principle in Judaism historically is belief in God's direct revelation of the written Torah (the first five books of Tanakh) together with an extensive framework of the exegetical rules for interpreting the commandments and specific instructions for their practical application. The mitzvot are traditionally numbered as 613 individual commandments, and they attend to nearly every aspect of daily, yearly, life cycle and ritual life. These include ceremonial rights and laws of family purity; rules governing criminal law, torts and civil law; ultimately, even a complicated and elusive instruction for the future creation of a monarchy. The body of interpretation, including both the rules of exegesis and the literal instructions for implementation of the mitzvot, are also understood from a traditional perspective to have been given directly from God to Moses during a 40 day process of revelation, a private dialogue between the Divine and his chosen prophet at the top of Mount Sinai.

The Mitzvot and the Torah

The collection of mitzvoth in the text of the Torah itself, referred to as the Torah Shebichtav (the written Torah) and the body of interpretation referred to as the Torah Sheba'al Peh (the oral Torah), were regarded by Jews before the end of the eighteenth century (and up to the present day among Orthodox Jews) as having equal authority. Both were understood as having been given directly by God to Moses at Sinai. The oral Torah was precisely that—orally transmitted—for a significant period of the early history of the Jewish religion. Indeed, one finds many traces of an oppositional attitude towards putting the contents of the oral Torah in writing. Within the rabbinic tradition, its transmission is regarded as unbroken and complete from Moses to the present day.

The primary method of transmission in the ancient period was encyclopedic memorization of the laws and the various opinions expressed in different meetings of the rabbinical academy, the Sanhedrin. This was a specialized skill, and individuals with particularly prodigious memories and recall, the tannaim, were valued sources, effectively living reference works in rabbinic debates over points of law. In this culture, the authority of interpretation was restricted through strict guidelines as to who demonstrated mastery of the methods of exegesis and knowledge of the Mesorah (tradition), the corpus of written and oral law. Rabbis taught in a master-apprentice style pedagogy, and their expertise was ritualized through the process of semicha, literally "placing [of hands] upon" the adept by his teacher as confirmation of his competence in halakhic knowledge. Rabbinic culture was entirely male, although the wife of the sage Rebbe Meir, Beruriah, appears to have had some standing as a halakhic opinion maker.

Picture 3. Model of Jerusalem during the Second Temple Period, Israel Museum, Jerusalem. The Temple grounds are the large structure at center. The Temple itself the tall building in its left-center

The crucial turning point in the development of Judaism was the destruction of the cultic center of worship in Jerusalem, the second Temple, by the

Roman army in 70 CE. While rabbis had eschewed the recording of Torah Sheba'al Peh, now its written preservation became a matter of cultural survival. The first written collection, which formed the core of rabbinic texts, was referred to as the Mishnah (literally "teaching") and contains verbatim recording of various authoritative teachings on each point of Torah law. Judah ha-Nasi, who tradition understands as the chief codifier of the Mishnah, included only a portion of the massive body of rabbinic material. Some of this material was redacted in other forms, such as the Tosefta (literally, "additions"). Other collections of rabbinic teachings dating from the classical period of Jewish history include aggregations of rabbinic homilies, called midrash. Also an integral literary form in the canon of the Talmud itself, midrash are discrete narrative vignettes attributed to individual rabbis. Often fantastical, these explorations of Biblical interpretation stretch far beyond straightforward legalistic clarification and instruction into astonishing fabulism and fantasy to illustrate legal, moral and communal principles.

Further afield from the rabbinic center of ancient Jewish literature are collections of Biblical texts, apocrypha and pseudepigrapha that emerged parallel to rabbinic literature. The most famous of these due to their sensational discovery in Israel in 1948 are a set of texts referred to as the Dead Sea Scrolls or Qumran manuscripts (Qumran referring to the location of the religious, quasi-monastic community that produced the manuscripts). In addition to providing variant ancient copies of canonized Biblical texts, these manuscripts contain texts that developed in parallel with early rabbinic Judaism. They give tantalizing but incomplete hints of the larger textual culture out of which the Jewish literary tradition emerged.

The completion of the Mishnah in the second century CE was only the beginning of the long process of interpretation and codification of the minutiae of Jewish law. Over the next few centuries with the Mishnah as the core, rabbinic scholars began further elucidation and interpretation of the text. These elucidations, which themselves were eventually collected, redacted and codified into a body of text referred to as the "Gemara," appeared in two forms. The first, referred to traditionally as the "Bavli," or Babylonian Talmud, would eventually become the central devotional Jewish text outside of the Torah itself. It was produced in the exiled communities in the Assyrian Empire, particularly in the academies of Sura and Pumbedita. This massive project utilized the same form of debate and exegesis as the Mishnah, and was compiled over several centuries; its final redaction occurred in approximately the sixth century. Illustrating the evolution of the Jewish community, the language of the Gemara (Aramaic, a widely-spoken vernacular of the period closely related to Hebrew) differs from that of the Mishnah (written in Hebrew, the language of Tanakh). Although closely related, the two languages differ in vocabulary and syntax. A second Gemara was produced at the same time as the Bavli, but its redaction ceased earlier and thus appeared as a less exhaustive compendium. This text, referred to traditionally as the "Yerushalmi," or Jerusalem (or "Palestinian") Talmud, although written in the same language as the Bavli, is wider in the scope of materials examined, yet much more succinct and cursory in its depth. Additionally, the Yerushalmi is an important source of ancient liturgical poetry, called piyyut, as well as a significant repository of unique midrashic (homelitic) literature.

The Talmud and the Triumph of Rabbinic Culture

The redaction of the Talmud was completed in the sixth century CE in the case of the Bavli, the fourth century CE in the case of the Yerushalmi. With this closure of what was now the core of the Jewish legal canon, so too ended the ancient rabbinic period. In the absence of any competing model or leadership that could survive without a cultic and political center, Judaism now became the religion of the rabbis.

The period of the redaction of the Talmud was followed by the period of the Geonim. At this point in Jewish history, which corresponds to the rise of

Islam in the regions of the world where the majority of Jews dwelt, authority in the Diaspora lay with the descendants of the editors of the Bavli. Under their influence, the religious literature devoted to explicating and interpreting Talmudic principle and law expanded extensively, and under their leadership the Talmud (Bavli) became entrenched in its place at the center of the Jewish literary canon as the definitive explication of the oral law alongside the written Torah. Geonic literature evolved a more coherent prose-form of discourse, which itself would be preserved until contemporary times (in Orthodox circles) as the style of responsa, or in Hebrew, Shaylot u-teshuvot literature.

Yet the core purpose of rabbinic literature remained largely unchanged: it was concerned with the interpretation and transmission of Jewish law, or as it had come to be called halakha, a term which literally means "way" or "path," referring to the "path" for correct observance of the Torah. At the same time, reflecting the influence of surrounding communities, other forms of Jewish literature began to appear, including philosophical tracts (such as the "The Book of Beliefs and Opinions" by Saadia Gaon). These texts directly reflect the considerable interaction of Jews and non-Jews in the early medieval period. Saadia Gaon's text, for instance, borrows from Greek philosophy (which was seeing a significant degree of copying, interpretation and study in this golden age of Islamic thought) and was written in Arabic, the language of both Saadia, his community, and the non-Jewish community in which they dwelt.

During the medieval period, the world Jewish population reached its maximum geographical dispersion in Europe, the Middle East, North Africa and Asia, and Jewish communities continued to develop in isolation that was bridged by bonds of religious connection and a robust epistolary culture —traits that would mark the Jewish world well into the modern era. Over time, the Geonic centers declined, while Jewish communities in other parts of the Islamic world—such as North Africa (the Maghreb) and the Iberian Peninsula—grew expansively. Other communities, mostly established during the late Roman Empire in Europe, began to represent a larger population and intellectual influence on the Diaspora. Finally, the Jewish community of the historical land of Israel was significantly reduced in its contribution to world Jewish culture. The Diaspora had become the primary locus of Jewish cultural development. And as the middle ages progressed, regional differences in Jewish culture, both material culture (dress, food, artisanal production) and religious culture widened.

After the decline of the Geonim in the Middle East, the tradition of religious literature entered into the period of the Rishonim, (literally "predecessors" or "first ones") corresponding roughly to the European early and high middle ages (approximately 800-1600 CE). Once again, the style and aims of rabbinic literature entered a new phase.

Reflecting the still robust religious and cultural links between Jews across the Diaspora, and at the same time the increasing diversity of the Jewish communities in different regions, literary culture in the Jewish world centered on the explication and understanding of the text, both as an end in itself and for understanding the correct practical application of halakha. Among the former, the medieval period saw perhaps the most vibrant flowering of Biblical exegesis among the meforshim (biblical commentators) of the Rhine Valley, Provence and the Iberian Peninsula. The most famous, and still widely consulted exegete was Rabbi Shlomo Yitzkhak, or Rashi, whose elegantly succinct commentary still adorns the standard page of the traditionally-printed Chumash (the printed Torah).

The Centrality of Jewish Legal Literature

The second major area of literary production sought to definitively codify halakha, which became the standard of greatness among the intellectual leadership across the Jewish world. Each attempt had the same goal: to digest and make comprehensible, clear and useful the complex and often confounding, even linguistically inaccessible guidance of the Talmud to a wider audience. As faithful observation of the halakha had become the determinant of Jewish identity, it was considered of the utmost importance to make this observance as clear as possible to as wide an audience capable of understanding it, and the stakes were very high —as reflected in the often vitriolic disputes between rabbis over disseminated halakhic digests.

The most famous early attempt at such codification was the work of famed Spanish (later Egyptian) rabbi and philosopher, Moses Maimonides (referred to commonly as the Rambam). Informed by his engagement with Arabic philosophy and its transmission of Aristotle, Maimonides organized a rationally-structured legal code, the *Mishneh Torah*, whose presence in halakhic literature looms so large that it is colloquially referred to as "the Rambam" or simply "the code." A later, but ultimately more successful and far more widely authoritative code of the halakha is the *Shulkhan Arukh* (the Set Table) of Joseph Caro. This text utilized a different basic structure than the *Mishneh Torah*, yet preserved the ideal of presenting an ordered, useful and definitive collection of the halakha. Not long after Caro released his work, Ashkenazi rabbi Moses Isserles (known as Rema) edited the text to include variant opinions relevant to his community (Caro, working in Safed, was of Sephardi extraction). Thus, shortly after its completion in the sixteenth century, the *Shulkhan Arukh* became, and has remained, the

ultimate codification of Jewish law. To this day, in
the Orthodox world, rabbis are ordained according
to their mastery of its different sections.

Although this tradition of halakhic literature
occupies pride of place as the center of Jewish religious
literature historically, it is not the only genre. Jews
participated in parallel with each division and genre
of literature as they emerged in broader European,
Mediterranean and Middle Eastern societies. The
philosophical works of Saadia Gaon and Maimonides
(in his monumental philosophical work *Moreh
Nevukhim*, Guide for the Perplexed) participated in
broader philosophical discussions—even writing in
the shared classical Arabic of the surrounding elite
literary culture. In addition to these formidable
philosophical edifices, rabbinic contributions (and
almost all contributions to Jewish literature that
survive before the modern era are rabbinic) include
a significant ethical literature, referred to as *musar*
(ethics). These practical texts are in wide use in some
circles as devotional texts to the present day. Other
genres, including poetry, such as the work of perhaps
the most famous Jewish figure in world medieval
literature, Yehudah ha-Levi, formed an important
contribution to the development of world literature
in the middle ages, often preserved and recited to this
day in the synagogue.

But perhaps the most significant genre of Jewish
literature situated outside of the mainstream of
rabbinic literature is the extensive collection of

esoteric literature commonly referred to as Kabbalah (literally "received" tradition). Deeply interwoven with oral literature of the rabbinic period and originating among the some of the same figures, esoteric Jewish literature represents a veritable alternate tradition of Jewish thought. Kabbalists and enthusiasts of esoterica themselves understand the tradition to have been received by Moses at Sinai like the oral Torah. In fact, the oldest known Kabbalistic literature dates to the period of the Mishnah, although traces of older elements do exist.

The work of Rabbi Isaac Luria (the Arizal) and his colleagues in sixteenth century Safed was the most important development in mystical thought in the modern period. While initially transmitted orally within small conventicles of adepts, Luria's ideas were eventually written and disseminated widely, which revolutionized the practice of Judaism. In addition to significant areas of addition and reorientation of liturgy and practice, Lurianic Kabbalah played an essential role in the emergence of both a massive popular movement that evolved into a monumental seventeenth century heresy (the messianic movement of Shabbatai Tzvi) and one of the most successful pietistic movements in modern Jewish history, Hasidism. This final turn, in the literature of the Kabbalistically-inclined Hasidic community that began in the mid-eighteenth century, has brought this esoteric literature up to the present day. Hasidic communities adhere closely to the mystical tradition of their Tsaddikim, or rabbinic leaders, and the most vibrant continued contribution to this literature in the period after the eighteenth century exists in the Hasidic world.

From Text to Practice

While the textual tradition outlined above forms the intellectual core of Judaism, there has always been a gap between the ideals of Judaism and its practice. So how is it practiced among individuals and in communities?

Judaism is a *communal* religion. It is not conceivable to practice Judaism in isolation from other Jews. At the same time, the core of historical Judaism—the observance of the *mitzvot* as divinely revealed to the Jewish people—governs both personal and public behavior. This interplay of the community and the individual, framed in terms of obligation to perfectly fulfill divine ordinances through both individual behavior and public communal rituals was present in the religion from its inception. Although current academic and archeological research has added a great deal of complexity to our understanding of how and under what circumstances ancient Judaism may have originated, this dynamic of public/private, communal/individual—an intertwining of the personal obligation and communal obligation—is consistent.

The central location of communal practice is the synagogue. What constitutes a synagogue varies from small prayer rooms to massive public buildings. The central ritual of public observance is the recitation of devotional texts codified by the rabbinic tradition (for the most part very early in its development —the time of the Mishnah, that is second century CE) and the public reading of the text of the Torah from a hand-written scroll. All other accoutrements— daily and weekly variations, additional devotional texts, variant prayers and readings on holidays—are layered on top of this basic structure.

In traditional communities, communal observance is daily and regarded as obligatory (even if often observed more in the breach) for all Jewish men above the age of thirteen. Men are enjoined to pray three times a day with a quorum of ten, referred to as a minyan. Some prayers, among them considered the most important in the liturgy, can only be recited with ten men (in Orthodox circles) or ten Jewish adults (in liberal circles). One of these is the centerpiece of each service, the Amidah ("standing prayer," so called because it is recited while standing stationary), otherwise known as the Shemona Esrei (literally "eighteen" blessings—after the number of discreet petitions originally contained in the weekday prayer). The other is the "sanctification" prayer, the Kaddish, which mourners are required to recite daily for eleven months after the death of a close family member. Even modern denominations of Judaism, which have adopted variations on this practice—such as extending the obligation to pray with a community to women and thus including them in the counting of a quorum—retain this basic structure.

What is this structure based upon? Every aspect of the public practice of Judaism either has its antecedent in or is a metaphor for elements of the original, ancient practices of the Israelites. The centerpiece of early Judaism was animal sacrifice at a single, designated center. In meticulous detail, the Torah describes a collection of rituals, ritual objects and their usage in daily public animal sacrifice. In the initial wanderings after the exodus from Egypt, the cultic center was the Mishkan (Tabernacle). The Mishkan was a tent-like complex, described in the text as the "dwelling place" of God. This ambiguous phrase is understood in different ways by different Jewish groups, from the most common understanding as metaphorical (although this may reflect later theological developments), to mystical understanding which preserves the ideal literally with a complex mystical cosmology. Its basic structure was maintained when the physical location of sacrifice was fixed at what Jews refer to as the Har Habayit (the Temple Mount) in Jerusalem, as the Bible describes it. At various moments in Biblical history, the exclusive sanctity of Jerusalem for conducting sacrifices was ambiguous. One form of decentralized sacrifice were the bamot, or sacrificial altars outside of the Temple in Jerusalem. Another instance is in the case of the Samaritans (Shomronim), whose tradition to this day identifies the sacred mountain in a different location (Har Hagerizim, currently in the northern West Bank).

As the Israelite community grew in size and evolved into a centralized monarchy, a grand Temple structure was erected by Solomon, which cemented both the connection of the monarchy with the Temple and centralized royal authority over religious practice. From that point on, the Temple was understood as the exclusive center of ritual, and presence in person or by assigned proxy at the Temple at least a few times a year (in particular during the three "pilgrimage holidays" of Pesach, Shavuot and Sukkot—see below) was required to fulfill one's religious obligations. Reflecting the theological hierarchy of the Torah, the Temple was administered by a priestly caste. The Kohanim, priests, were charged with the actual administration of sacrifice and its attendant rituals, the Leviim, or Levites, carried out supporting administrative and ritual tasks that supported the priest's primary work of offering sacrifices.

The Torah describes in great detail the rules of animal sacrifice as well as the ritual objects that were central to the Temple service, which would become the most identifiable symbols of Judaism. The central objects were those understood to represent the primary symbols of the covenant with God, which were kept in the sacred center of the Mishkan (and later the Temple), a chamber referred to as the "Holy of Holies" (Kadosh-kadoshim). The Holy of Holies contained the Aron Hakodesh (the Holy Ark), a large casket encased in gold to precise specifications recorded in the Torah, which traditionally was understood to contain the tablets, written with the finger of God, handed to Moses at Sinai. It was generally forbidden to enter the chamber, whose innermost section was separated off by a special curtain (parokhet) and entered only once a year, at the height of the observance of Yom Kippur (the Day of Atonement, see below), and only by the chief priest (Kohen Gadol).

The rest of the accoutrements of the Mishkan were dedicated to serving specific functions in the daily service of sacrifices processed by the kohanim. Some of these objects include the mizbeach (altar) which was the primary physical location of animal sacrifice, and the menorah (a seven-branched candelabra that stood on the south side of the altar). On normal weekdays (Sunday through Friday), sacrifices were organized around a rigorous schedule and the proper execution of the process in its appointed time was regarded of paramount importance, with severe physical and spiritual penalties imposed on priests who erred in performing their duties.

On Shabbat and holidays, including Rosh Hashanah, Yom Kippur, and the three pilgrimage holidays, additional sacrifices were added to the daily schedule. On Rosh Hashanah and the holidays, there was an additional sacrificial service (musaf, the "additional service") and on Yom Kippur, even other sacrifices were offered. Individuals were responsible for purchasing and bringing (or appointing an emissary to bring) animals, which included cattle, sheep, and small fowl and flour, which were then slaughtered or prepared by the kohanim. These sacrifices served specific purposes and were designated as such, including sacrifices to atone for sin, to offer thanksgiving for good fortune, and other purposes in addition to the obligatory required daily offerings.

Although the Israelite religion was fundamentally altered by the destruction of both Temples and the exile of the Jewish people from the land, the idea of the Temple remained an essential part of Judaism in rabbinic literature. Both editions of the Talmud retain an extensive record of the specific laws of the Temple sacrifices, architecture, and vessels. These post-destruction texts preserve in exacting detail the complex issues of priestly purity, allowed and prohibited relations between kohanim and non-priests. The process was intended in part to keep the requisite knowledge alive. After the Roman conquest, it became central to Jewish belief faith that the Temple could be miraculously rebuilt at any moment, and the Jewish people must be prepared to resume the "proper" worship of God. When a later revolt (the Bar Kokhba revolt in 132-135 CE) resulted in the aggressive suppression of remaining Jewish practice in its heartland, this compulsion to preserve became even more important.

One result of this was the transformation of the elements of ritual sacrifice into symbolic form. Many historians and modern Jewish theologians have argued that this symbolization was a sublimation, an ascent to a higher level of religious sensibility from the physical (actual material sacrifice) to the spiritual (symbolic re-enactment of sacrifice in elements of non-sacrificial ritual practice). It is more likely (and remains traditional position) that these symbolic enactments are not replacements, but merely placeholders for an eventual reconstruction of the Temple and resumption of the practice of ancient Judaism as the Torah describes it. Evidence for this is the fact that many of the practices that filled the vacuum left by the myriad obligations related to sacrifice were already in place before the Temple's destruction. Much of the liturgy, which remains fairly consistent across Jewish denominations in its structure, existed in a familiar form *before* the destruction of the Temple, as did the physical centers of worship which would, after the Temple's destruction, become the locus of Jewish practice: the synagogue.

The Synagogue and Jewish Prayer

The Ancient Origins of the Synagogue

The basic form of the synagogue existed before the destruction of the Second Temple, and the ruins of ancient synagogues with a structure similar to those throughout the Jewish world to this day can be easily found in present-day Israel. This is familiar to readers of the Christian Bible as specific anecdotes related to the life of Jesus reference synagogues, such as that of Capernaum on the Kineret (Sea of Galilee). Others, including those in Galilee such as that at Magdala and in other locations such as among the ruins of Masada indicate that daily, communal ritual practice away from the Temple service was already a normal element of Judaism before the Temple's destruction.

While the external aesthetic appearance of the synagogue varies across Jewish history and is usually influenced by the tastes of the surrounding cultures, the interior layout of most synagogues is strikingly consistent. The central chamber of the synagogue, usually referred to in modern terms as the "sanctuary," is a room, usually rectangular. At one end is a large cabinet, often ornate and dominating the space of the wall against which it is built, the Aron ha-kodesh (the holy ark), which contains the hand-written Torah scrolls. Usually a communal synagogue will have several, for as many as three may be required ritually at one time. Most often, the ark is in an elevated position, with stairs leading up to it that are ascended and descended during the ritual removal of the Torah scrolls when they are read. The Torah is publically read in the synagogue four times a week: Monday and Thursday morning, Saturday morning and afternoon.

The ark is usually covered by a parokhet (curtain) which is often intricately decorated. The central feature is the bimah (platform or stage). Traditionally the bimah was located in the middle of the synagogue chamber, and in ancient and medieval synagogues, it is not uncommon to see the bimah take up a quarter or more of the floor space of the room. In more modern synagogues (of all denominations), it is not uncommon to see the bimah at the front of the room, directly in front of the aron. Atop the bimah is a large reading table, the shulkhan (table), from which the Torah is publicly read. Each of these fixtures of the synagogue are intended to evoke the Temple service: the aron as a stand-in for the Holy of Holies with the original aron inside, the bimah and shulkhan for the altar that stood in the courtyard of the Temple, the parokhet for the sacred curtain shielding the Holy of Holies. The leader of services, referred to traditionally as the ba'al tefillah (the prayer leader) or shaliach tzibbur (the messenger of the community) is compared to the High Priest, a connection that is made explicit in the Yom Kippur liturgy.

As the liturgy evolved into its basic form in the rabbinic period, it remained, like other rabbinic literature, oral. Although the skeleton of the rabbinic liturgy is present in the Mishnah, its complete formulation did not occur until after the destruction of the Second Temple. During the ancient period, prayers were recited from memory in public, and for those who did not have comprehensive knowledge of the prayers, they were recited aloud by the precentor, and the answer of "Amen" was considered as though the supplicant had recited the blessing themselves. This is still the practice in traditional synagogues today.

The first comprehensive siddur (prayerbook), the *Seder Rav Amram Gaon*, appeared among the Geonim around the ninth century CE. The *Mahzor Vitri*, the template for the structure and contents of the prayerbook afterwards, emerged in the eleventh century in the Ashkenazi community of the Rhineland in Europe. For the most part, the prayerbook has maintained a remarkable consistency in its construction. All prayerbooks contain the central "skeleton" of the Jewish liturgy—the blessings required for a Jew to fulfill all mitzvot relevant to daily life, the extended blessings of the Shema (see below) and the 18 blessings of the Shemona Esrei or Amidah, and the seasonal variations including festivals and holidays.

Picture 4. "The Altneushul (Old-New Synagogue) in Prague. This thirteenth-century structure shows the influence of surrounding culture in synagogue design and architecture."

The arrival of the printing press in the fifteenth century further standardized the siddur regionally, and gradually a few different "rites" came to dominate the majority of communities. By the modern period (post-seventeenth century), there were two primary forms of the prayerbook with many local variations that emerged as the Ashkenazi and Sephardi or Mizrahi form. One further permutation of the traditional prayerbook occurred in the eighteenth century with the emergence of modern Hasidim (a pietistic faction that dominated many communities in Poland, Ukraine and Belorussia) which utilized the mystical theories of the Sephardi rabbi R. Isaac Luria (traditionally referred to as the "Arizal") as a guideline to join elements of the Mizrahi and Ashkenazi rites into a new rite, the *Siddur Ha-Ari*, or the *Nusach Sefard*, which in its basic form has also become the standard siddur in most Ashkenazi Israeli synagogues in the late modern period.

As modernization accelerated in European Jewish communities in the nineteenth century, the contents of the prayerbook became a central point of contention dividing traditionalists and modernizers. Numerous editions of the siddur appeared in central Europe, western Europe and North America, each of which made editorial decisions on material that would be included and excluded for modern congregations. For the first time since the rabbinic period, significant changes were made to the actual text of the core blessings. These changes, which were roundly rejected by traditionalists (who, by the 1840s, began to use the designation "Orthodox" to distinguish themselves from "Reform" modernizers) sought to re-orient the ancient text of the siddur in accordance with modern tastes and attitudes. References to animal sacrifice were elided, as were references to the re-establishment of the Jewish commonwealth and Davidic kingdom, which were regarded as irrelevant to modern European Jews.

By the twentieth century, especially in European and American congregations, the prayerbook become even more standardized. Denominational groups, which in the United States included the Reform, Conservative, the Reconstructionist movement, and mainstream Orthodoxy developed their own standardized version of the prayerbook. In Orthodoxy, where there is no central board or governing authority, the use of a standard prayerbook in many congregations emerged as a result of popular consensus, and individuals and communities use a wide variation of *siddurim*. In regions with a centralized rabbinic authority (such as the United Kingdom, Israel and France), the governing body, usually a chief rabbinate, oversees an authorized version of the prayerbook, which is in use in congregations affiliated with the rabbinate, although independent congregations may or may not utilize it. Even among the most dramatic changes in modern times, the siddur of all groups is still organized around the thrice-daily liturgy that is traditionally intended to be recited by all adult Jewish males, and in modernized congregations, all Jewish adults.

As mentioned, the core of this liturgy is the combination of prayers referred to as the Shema and the Shemona Esrei or Amidah. The Shema is the central part of the Jewish liturgy; its recitation twice daily is the cornerstone of the liturgy and its textual origin is the Torah itself. It is composed of a collection of verses from the Torah which declaim the unity of God ("Hear, O Israel, the Lord is your God, the Lord is One") along with three passages, also from the Torah, which detail the obligation to acknowledge the unity of God twice daily, as well as the other ritual obligations connected to the concept of God's unity, including the obligation to post the commandment on door and gateposts (*mezuzah*), to physically attach the words to the body twice daily (*tefillin*), and to instruct children of this core belief. Finally, a third passage is recited which seemingly adds a historical dimension to the prayer, which commands Jewish men to attach tzitzit (fringes) to the "corners of their garments" to serve as a reminder of the redemption from Egypt, the central founding story of the Jewish people.

Each of the elements mentioned in the Shema —mezuzah, tefillin, and tzitzit—are considered literal obligations by Orthodox Jews, although many non-Orthodox Jews also observe them. Mezuzot are comprised of a hand-written parchment scroll with the paragraphs of the Shema that mention the commandment to post the "these words," (i.e., the words of the commandment) on doorposts, and a decorative cover which protects the scroll from the elements. Tefillin (phylacteries) are two rigid leather boxes, one worn on the arm, the other on the forehead, attached with black leather straps which are wrapped and tied in a prescribed pattern. Inside the boxes, in one chamber in the tefillah shel yad (arm tefillah) and four chambers in the tefillah shel rosh (head tefillah) contain scrolls of parchment inscribed (again, by hand) with the four paragraphs that mention tefillin in the Torah. Men in the Orthodox world are commanded to "lay" tefillin every morning as part of the morning liturgy, and some women have also made it their practice within the Orthodox world (although this is a contentious issue in that community), and more widely in non-Orthodox congregations. Finally, tzitzit (ritual fringes) are threads tied in a prescribed pattern that men are required to attach to four-cornered garments. While Orthodox men will wear a tallit katan (a four-cornered undergarment with tzitzit) under their clothing at all times, most male Jews who attend synagogue of any denomination will don a large four-cornered tallit gadol (prayer shawl) for morning prayers. In liberal denominations, it is also not uncommon for women to wear a tallit at prayer.

In the morning and evening services, the Shema is recited and connected via thematic blessings to the Amidah. The afternoon service, Mincha, is composed mostly of the Amidah and does not contain the shema. Composed of nineteen discreet blessings or petitions, the formulation of which occurred during the Second Temple period, the Amidah contains the central expressions of the Jewish theological understanding of the relationship between God and the individual, the Jewish community, and a specific attitude and understanding of Jewish history. The first three blessings, which include a ubiquitous formula and opening clause ("Blessed are You, God, sovereign of the universe, God of Abraham, God of Isaac, God of Jacob"), establish the conception of the divine as unique and unified, as the guarantor of the Jewish people's redemption, whose essence is pure holiness (or Kedusha). In prayer services when the prayer is recited out loud, an extension of the third "Kedusha" blessing is recited responsively by the preceptor and the congregation. The next thirteen blessings are petitionary, dealing with issues from prayer for health, for good livelihood, to remembrance of martyrs and other righteous individuals, request for the forgiveness of sins, for the acquisition of knowledge, condemnation of heretics, the ingathering of the exiles, the restoration of sacrifices and rebuilding of the Temple. Finally, the "chatimah" or "sealing" of the prayer includes four parts. These include a blessing of thanksgiving, a recitation (during the oral repetition of the prayer) of the blessings recited by the Kohanim for the rest of the Jewish people, a final plea for the re-establishment of Jewish sovereignty in the historical land of Israel, and finally a blessing requesting universal peace and brotherhood. On Shabbat and festivals other than Rosh Hashanah and Yom Kippur, the middle thirteen blessings are omitted and replaced with prayers whose purpose is to reiterate the sanctity of the holiday.

Reading the Torah is another central element of public Jewish worship. It is read in public four times a week: on Monday and Thursday mornings, and during Shabbat morning and afternoon services. The public reading is woven into the fabric of the liturgy, after the Amidah in the morning services, and before it in the afternoon service. For the sake of public reading, the Torah is divided into fifty-four separate sections, or parshiot, which are read in a yearly cycle. In traditional congregations, this allows for the entire Torah to be read publicly, from a hand-written scroll (which is required), each year. In some liberal congregations, a triennial model is followed, where the Torah is completed once every three years. In each separate, "special" service, such as those of holidays, fast days and new months (Rosh Hodesh), set sections of the Torah that reference the holiday and its sacrifices are read in place of the weekly parshiot. On Shabbat, fast days and other festivals, a set section of the prophetic books of the Bible are read, referred to as the weekly Haftorah, generally arranged with thematic connection to the weekly parsha. Finally, on certain festival and sub-festival days, including Passover, Sukkot, Tisha B'Av, Purim, and Shavuot, each of the megillot are read corresponding to the themes of the day (see below in discussion of holidays).

In addition to the Shema and the Amidah, the structure of Jewish liturgy has been elaborated and added to over the entirety of post-Temple Jewish history. For the most part, Orthodox siddurim retain the bulk of accumulated liturgical material as part of the daily service. In other denominations, much of this material has been omitted, although the American Conservative movement (referred to as "Masorti" outside of the United States) retains content similar to an Orthodox synagogue in practice. This material includes: a number of blessings, recitations of sections of Torah and other biblical writings, rabbinic formulae and sections from rabbinic literature, liturgic poetry (*piyyut*) primarily originating in the middle ages, and accretions of later rabbinic texts associated with the esoterica of the Kabbalah.

Shabbat and the Jewish Year

Centrality of Shabbat as a Sanctified Day

Time in Judaism can be understood in terms of a circular pattern of holidays over the course of the year, beginning with the first divinely-ordained holiday, Shabbat. The command that Israelites refrain from all work for a twenty-five hour period on the seventh day of the week is described in the sources as a living memory to God's creation of the world described in the opening of the Torah itself, and is the cornerstone (and paradigm) of the traditional sanctification of the passage of time in Jewish life.

In line with the literal description of time in the Torah's creation story, Shabbat (and all other days of the week) is considered to begin at sundown of the previous day; thus the first prayer service of Shabbat is ma'ariv, the evening prayer. While the Torah prohibits labor on Shabbat, requiring a full day of rest in imitation of God's own rest after the first six days of creation, the meaning of this is explicated by the sages of the Talmud as comprising thirty-nine prohibited categories of work, all of which are derived from the specific tasks related to the construction of the Mishkan. To this day these prohibitions continue to be observed punctiliously in Orthodox communities and among many who do not define themselves as Orthodox. This, of course, has significant implications for the lifestyles of individuals and the structure of Jewish communities. Restrictions on travel by means other than walking require Shabbat-observant Jews to live in areas concentrated around religious infrastructure such as synagogues and mikvah (ritual bath). This, in turn, creates a strong sense of collectivity and community, which is itself an important component of Shabbat and holiday observance.

Shabbat is a central pillar of Jewish identity for traditionally-observant Jews and those who observe modernized practice alike. The day is customarily devoted to prayer, celebratory food and drink, and community. After communal prayer, traditionally families and friends gather for the first of three obligatory "festive meals," (seudah), which is sanctified through the rabbinic formula of Kiddush (sanctification) over a glass of wine. The rest of the day is spent engaged in other leisurely pursuits that do not involve violation of the laws governing work (melakha) on Shabbat; many individuals heighten their study of the Torah and other devotional texts. Finally, in the late afternoon the community gathers again for the afternoon prayer (in Orthodox communities, usually it is men only who attend Shabbat minchah), and the third obligatory seudah, followed by the ending of Shabbat and the recitation of the weekday evening prayer. A formal ceremony, Havdalah (separation) is recited over a cup of wine, spices and a multi-wicked candle. The wine, as with Kiddush, serves as the formal object of sanctification of the moment; the pleasant aroma of spices represents the departure of the "Shabbat soul" that, according to kabbalists, each Jew acquires on Shabbat and which departs at the end of the day. Finally, the multi-wicked candle (the lighting of which is disallowed on Shabbat itself) represents the renewal of the week, the beginning once more of creative work until the next Shabbat.

The cyclical structure of the Jewish calendar continues in the next significant temporal marker: Rosh Hodesh, the new month. Unlike the western calendar but similar to that of Islam, the Jewish calendar is lunar, following a twelve year cycle of twelve and thirteen months of twenty-nine or thirty

days (in a "leap year," the month Adar is observed
twice). Although the calendar was fixed using
mathematical calculation in the fourth century CE, in
ancient Israel the new month was announced based
upon lunar observation from Jerusalem. Because
of the time taken to announce the new moon over
long distance, and the importance from a halakhic
perspective of performing the commandments
related to the date at their appropriate time, the rabbis
created a safeguard to prevent mistakes: outside
of Israel the three festival holidays (see below), are
celebrated for two consecutive days rather than one.
The twelve months of the Hebrew calendar are (in
order from Rosh Hashanah, which usually occurs in
the month of September): Tishrei, Heshvan, Kislev,
Tevet, Shevet, Adar (and Adar II in a leap year),
Nissan, Iyar, Sivan, Tammuz, Av, and Elul.

The other Jewish holidays fall under three general
designations. The first are the two holidays centering
on repentance (teshuva) and yearly atonement, the
Yomim Noraim (Days of Awe), Rosh Hashanah and
Yom Kippur, which occur in the autumn month of
Tishrei. The next category of Jewish holidays are the
festival holidays (hagim or yomim tovim), holidays
including Pesach, Shavuot and Sukkot, which correlate
to both the history of ancient Israel as an agricultural
society and the yearly remembrance of central events in
its religious history, especially the commemoration of
the redemption from Egypt. Each of these holidays has
the status of a full yom tov, marked by restrictions on

work similar to Shabbat (or, in the case of Yom Kippur, regarded as the "Shabbat shabbaton," the "Sabbath of Sabbaths"). Next are minor holidays commemorating specific historical events in ancient Jewish history. These holidays, including Hanukkah, Purim, and the Ninth of Av, do have specific rituals, but not the same prohibition of work and which are, for the most part, later rabbinic additions to the calendar.

The Yamim Noraim

Although all of the major holidays are regarded as having unique sanctity, two stand out in their devotional significance: Rosh Hashanah (New Year) and Yom Kippur (day of atonement or judgement), the central pillars of a period of collective repentance and introspection.

Beginning on the first day of the Hebrew month Tishrei (falling in late September or early October), the Torah commands the Jewish people to sound the shofar to initiate the process of seeking repentance by the collective Jewish people. The shofar—a hollowed ram's horn—is blown by a congregant for one hundred individual blasts, accompanied by a specific recital of prayers and blessings. The main themes of the holiday are the call to repentance, the acknowledgement of God as the sovereign of the universe, and reflection on the creation of the world

—all of which are described in detail as part of the Rosh Hashanah liturgy. It is also believed that these days begin in earnest the divine adjudication of guilt and innocence of all Jews that culminates in Yom Kippur. Like other major holidays, Jews are enjoined from labor on both days of Rosh Hashanah.

Following Rosh Hashanah are ten days that are considered of heightened importance in the process of Jews' reflection on their behavior over the past year, the Aseret Yemei Teshuva (ten days of repentance). During these days Jews traditionally engage in reflection, additional prayers (referred to as selichot, "petitions" for forgiveness) which are also recited in the days leading up to Rosh Hashanah itself, as well as the efforts to make amends to others for offenses committed over the year.

The culmination of the teshuva period is the holiday of Yom Kippur. Referred to in the Torah as the Shabbat Shabbaton, the "Sabbath of Sabbaths," Yom Kippur has the same technical restrictions on work as Shabbat. In addition, Jews refrain from eating and drinking, sexual relations, anointing the body with oils or perfume, and wearing leather shoes. The Torah places significant emphasis on the rituals of Yom Kippur. The heightened sanctity of the day is emphasized throughout the Torah and rabbinic literature, and it is one of the most widely observed holidays by Jews of every denomination and identity. Yom Kippur begins with the recitation of the Kol Nidre prayer, an Aramaic text which formally absolves the community of oaths made to God in error. In traditional circles, men will wear a "kittel," a white robe, and in all expressions of Judaism the color white is widely worn by both men and women, symbolizing the purification of the Jews as they enter into the day of Judgement. Judgement is the primary theme of the day, as the number of prayers are extended to include extensive selichot (poetic petitions for forgiveness), as well as confessional formulations repeated throughout the day.

In the Biblical formulation and ancient observance of the day, which today is read in synagogue and enacted in various ways, Yom Kippur is an intense ordeal which centers on the activities of the kohen ha-gadol as he offers the requisite sacrifices outlined in the Torah. In addition to the normal daily and holiday sacrifices, the kohen gadol offers special sacrifices that are intended to atone for the collective sins of the Jewish people. Most familiar of these is the "scapegoat" ritual, described in detail in the text, wherein two goats are brought before the kohen gadol, lots are thrown to determine which goat will be sacrificed on the altar and which will be designated as the seir ha-mishtaleach (scapegoat) who is ritually guided out of the Temple grounds with a crimson thread tied around its neck, which matches crimson thread hanging in the Temple. The goat is chased to a high cliff (traditionally understood to have been Jebel Muntar, east of Jerusalem), where it is pushed to its death as the symbolic atonement for Israel's sins. Upon its death, according to tradition, the crimson thread suspended in the Temple would turn miraculously white, confirming God's acceptance of Israel's repentance.

In modern practice, Jews observe Yom Kippur through extensive prayer and a unique formula of confession (Viddui) as well as Torah readings tied to the events of the day, and one of the minor prophets, Jonah, whose entire story is read aloud in the afternoon service. The liturgy is long enough that the entire day is often occupied by prayer. It concludes with the unique Neilah prayer, an additional recitation of the Yom Kippur Amidah that is the final petition of the Jewish people before the Day of Judgement ends. The doors of the Torah arc close at the end, heralded with the blowing of the shofar, symbolizing the closure of the shaarei teshuva (gates of repentance).

The Three Festival Holidays

After Rosh Hashanah and Yom Kippur, the central holidays of the Jewish calendar are the "festival" holidays (shalosh regalim or yomim tovim): Pesach (Passover), Shavuot (Pentecost) and Sukkot (Feast of Booths). Each of these three holidays articulate different devotional themes tied to the historical experiences of the Biblical Israelites, and also functioned as the pilgrimage holidays tied to specific periods of the agricultural calendar in Biblical Israel. It was on these holidays that Jews were obligated to present themselves at the Temple to offer the sacrifices relevant to the holiday.

The first of these, perhaps the most central holiday on the Jewish calendar after Yom Kippur in its popular observance by contemporary Jews, is Pesach, Passover. The holiday falls on the fifteenth of Nissan (March or April). It marks the divine redemption of the Hebrews from Egyptian slavery, and is widely observed by Jews of all denominations and identities. The central rituals of the holiday described in the Torah involve a few key components. The first, as mentioned, was the obligation of aliyat ha-regel (pilgrimage to Jerusalem)—the individual was expected to be present at the Temple in observance of the holiday. Each family group of pilgrims brought their own paschal sacrifice—a lamb—which was slaughtered by the Cohen and roasted whole for consumption by each family group.

Once the sacrifice was offered, the other rituals of Pesach revolved around eating, drinking, and re-telling the story of the redemption from Egypt, a celebratory meal referred to as the seder (literally "order of events"). This re-telling, derived from the Biblical commandment to specifically recount the miraculous redemption and is discussed in more detail in the Mishnah, became very early on a standardized text of rabbinic and biblical material, blessings, and later liturgical poetry, the Haggadah. In addition to the texts of discussing the redemption specifically, the Haggadah contains the formulae, blessings and instructions for the process of the seder ritual which outlines precise structure and choreography for the performance of the seder. The specific mitzvot include the consumption of the paschal sacrifice, along with matzah (unleavened bread, carefully prepared with only flour and water, strictly timed and baked at high temperature to avoid any possibility of leavening) that is consumed by Jews over the entire length of the festival. In memory of the rapid departure of the Hebrews from Egyptian bondage, any products which may have been intentionally or unintentionally leavened in the process of their preparation are banned from consumption. Finally, the seder ritual requires drinking four glasses of wine at specific moments in the seder, to sanctify each discrete ritual component.

In the contemporary Jewish world, Pesach is observed by traditional practitioners for seven days, of which the first and last (first two and last two in the Diaspora, for a total of eight days) are full holidays with restrictions on labor similar to Shabbat. The intermediate days (again, generally observed only by those of traditional or Orthodox practice) are also considered to be of a heightened sanctity, referred to as hol ha-moed, the intermediate festival days. During these days, the overarching mitzvot of the festival are observed (for instance, on Pesach no unleavened products are consumed for the entire holiday, only matzah).

Seven weeks after the conclusion of Pesach, the second of the three shalosh regalim, Shavuot, is celebrated. Unlike the other two festival holidays,

Shavuot is observed for one day only (two in the Diaspora). In classical sources, the holiday contains an amalgam of different meanings. In the Torah, it is primarily agricultural, as is evident in the terms by which the holiday is referred: Shavuot, literally "weeks," referring to the seven weeks of sheaf (wheat) offerings brought from Pesach to Shavuot. As one of the trio of pilgrimage holidays, Jews were commanded to present themselves and their sacrifices at the Temple in Jerusalem. Over time, based upon rabbinic calculation of the unfolding of the redemption from Egypt, Shavuot became associated with the day of the revelation of the Torah to the Jewish people at Sinai. The enshrinement of Shavuot as the day of revelation became, after the destruction of the Temple, the dominant theme of the holiday.

Thus the focus of Shavuot is celebrating the Torah and the Jewish people's covenant with God. In addition to the additions to the festival liturgy (which refers to the holiday as "Zman Mattan Torateynu," "the time of the giving of our Torah"), the holiday is marked by an intensification of Torah study. Current practice often includes a leyl tikkun, an all-night session of Torah study, a Kabbalistic custom that was appended to the holiday fairly late in Jewish history. In the synagogue, in addition to the festival liturgy, the megillah Ruth is read in its entirety, a story which details the conversion of a Moabite woman to Judaism during the harvest season, thus unifying the different themes of the harvest and the embrace of Torah that are central to the holiday.

The last of the three festivals is the autumn harvest festival of Sukkot, usually translated as the "feast of booths." This holiday, like Pesach seven days long (eight in the Diaspora), is considered part of the larger autumn festival season due to its close proximity to Rosh Hashanah and Yom Kippur (it begins less than a week after Yom Kippur). Like Sukkot, the Biblical references to the holiday refer almost entirely to its agricultural significance. The Torah describes two specific obligations unique to the holiday: the "taking" of the arba minim (four species) and dwelling in the sukkah. The first of these, the arba minim, requires that Jews collect an etrog (citron), a lulav (young palm branch), a hadassim (laurel branches) and aravot (willow branches) in hand. While no specific direction is given as to how the objects are to be "taken," the ritual as practiced today first evolved in the rabbinic period, and has developed various accoutrements over time. In the basic ritual, the three branches are bound together and held in two hands together with the citron, and a blessing is recited acknowledging the commandment and waved in the four directions of the compass. This ritual has acquired many layers of significance, most connected to Kabbalistic interpretation which references the connection of the celebration of the holiday in the Temple. On each day of the festival, an extended ritual is performed by the congregation:

a procession around the center of the synagogue with the four species in hand, where distinguished members of the congregation hold the community's Torah scrolls, a ritual which is intended to evoke circuits made in the courtyard of the Temple. A special liturgy, Hoshannot (pleas for redemption), is recited while the congregation circulates. The final intermediate day of the festival is the culmination of this ritual, called Hoshannah Rabba (the great hosanah), which expands the circuits to seven circuits around the synagogue, again a later Kabbalistic practice.

The second Biblical obligation of Sukkot is the sukkah, or booth, itself. The Torah commands that each family group construct (or borrow) a temporary structure, outside of the home, that is covered by a roof of branches, sheaves or other vegetative material, and "dwell" in the sukkah for the entirety of the festival. The commandment to dwell is often observed in traditional communities literally— families, or at least male members, will eat, spend leisure time, and even sleep in the sukkah; the most common practice is to eat all formal meals (meals that include the consumption of grain products or bread) in the sukkah. These rituals embrace the dual themes of the agricultural cycle of the ancient Israelite year and the experience of the redemption from Egypt.

In addition to the major holidays and festivals on the Jewish calendar are the minor holidays: Hanukkah, Purim and Tisha b'Av. Unlike the major holidays, these three holidays are not mentioned in the Torah; all emerged in the rabbinic period, and the last, Tisha b'Av, around the destruction of the Second Temple. Additionally, each of these holidays contains a more significant "national" component than the Torah-mandated holidays. Each carries significance in their commemoration of a later triumph (or, in the case of Tisha b'Av, tragedy) encountered by the Jewish collective. Further, each is marked by a specific ritual of observance that was elevated by the rabbis to the level of obligatory mitzvah.

Hanukkah, an eight day festival which straddles the end of the winter month of Kislev and the beginning of Tevet (December), commemorates the victory during the Second Temple period of a Jewish revolt against the Hellenistic rule of Seleucid king Antiochus Epiphanes in the second century BCE (see chapter 3). Hanukkah is celebrated in honor of Judah Maccabee's entry into Jerusalem and re-consecration of the Temple and its altar (thus the name of the holiday, taken from Hanukkat ha-mizbeah, the sanctification of the altar). The primary obligation of the holiday is the lighting of the menorah or hanukkiah (candelabra), a reference to the sacred vessel in the Temple. It differs from the Temple's menorah as it has eight arms instead of six, for each of the days of the holiday. Other customs associated with the holiday are celebratory meals, and, in modern culture, the exchange of small gifts.

The second of the minor holidays, Purim, is celebrated on the 14th of Adar or the 15th of Adar in cities that are regarded as ancient, walled cities (usually in March). Like Hanukkah, Purim commemorates a moment of victory in Jewish history, this time in the Diaspora community of Persia during the Second Temple period. According to textual sources (primarily the megillah dedicated to the holiday itself, *Esther*, as well as a tractate of the Talmud), the holiday originated out of a moment of persecution of the Persian Diaspora community under a king referred to as Ahasuerus, understood to have ruled Persia at some point after Cyrus the Great. According to the story, which is chanted from the megillah on both the evening and morning of the holiday, the Jewish community was targeted for extermination by an evil counsellor of the king, Haman. Thanks to the intervention of a pious Jewish communal leader, who encourages his niece, Esther, to become part of Ahasuerus' harem in order to gain the ear of the king and upset Haman's plan, the plot is foiled, and instead of the Jews of Persia being murdered, they are given permission to kill Mordechai, his offspring and supporters. Historically speaking, the events recorded in Esther are impossible to substantiate (there is no clear consensus on who Ahasuerus was, for instance), but based upon the megillah itself and the Talmudic tractate dedicated to enumerating the laws of its observance, it is clear that the holiday was widely celebrated during the late Second Temple period.

The final of the minor historical holidays is Tisha b'Av, the Ninth of Av. Like the other two, it commemorates a later event in ancient Jewish history, but in this case a tragedy: the destruction of the Temple of Jerusalem. It is unclear how early Tisha b'Av was observed widely, but rabbinic tradition holds that both the first and second temples were destroyed on the ninth of Av. Tisha b'Av is the quintessential communal day of mourning the historical exile of the Jewish people from the land of Israel. For traditional Jews, and as understood by the rabbis of the Talmud, it is even more poignantly associated with the severed connection between the Jewish people and God that the loss of physical sacrifice represented. As codified in the Mishnah, and as currently practiced, observance of Tisha b'Av adapts the practices of mourning (see chapter 2) in addition to prohibiting eating and drinking. The megillah *Eichah* (Lamentations, attributed to the prophet Jeremiah), composed after the destruction of the first Temple, is read along with several kinot (lamentations) that detail the various travails of the Jewish people throughout history. Congregants, wearing non-leather shoes, sit on the floor or low stools as is customary in a house of mourning. In addition to consuming food and drink, traditional observation requires refraining from bathing, anointing with perfume, and sexual intercourse, similar to the restrictions on Yom Kippur.

Although the religious conception is perhaps the most ancient and continuously robust—as well as most widely acknowledged—cultural model of Jewish identity, it is but one of our three categories. And though it is essential to understand the religious foundation of Jewish identity, it is incomprehensible without understanding the two other forms of Jewish cultural identity, the culture of the community in its public and private forms, and the culture of the nation. Having laid the foundation for our encounter with Jewish culture through its extensive religious history, let us now turn to the world of the *actors* of that culture—the Jewish individual, family, and communal collective.

Chapter 2

Community and Family: Jewish Culture of the Private and Public Sphere

Judaism and the Jewish Family

While religion serves as the foundation and most visible expression of Jewish culture, it is in the family and the community that Jewish culture is lived. And in daily Jewish life, perhaps no concept is as important as the idea of the Jewish people as an extended family. In its most basic form, Judaism is understood by Jews as the historical religion of Abraham, his wife Sarah, and their descendants. The Torah conceptualizes the foundation of Judaism as a covenant between God and Abraham which explicitly guarantees the promises made to Abraham, the patriarch, as binding for his children and descendants so long as they maintain their loyalty to it. Three Biblical generations later, the clan grew into a collection of tribes based upon their descent from the original sons of Abraham's grandson, Jacob, a tribal structure which formed the basis for Israelite political organization once Moses led the exiled Israelites out of Egypt.

The existence of any distinct family-based tribes disappeared with the destruction of the first Temple, and with it the first iteration of Israelite sovereignty. Nevertheless, some practices based upon tribal distinction survive in Jewish rituals to the present day. One expression that survives is the distinction between "Israelites" and the Kohanim and Leviim, the priestly caste that had the exclusive obligation to perform the Temple service that formed the basis of the ancient Israelite religion. To this day, in Orthodox and traditional synagogues, it is the prerogative of the Kohanim to accept the first aliyah to the Torah (the first section of the portion read in synagogue each week), and the Leviim the second. A further remnant of this distinction, again mostly present in Orthodox and traditional synagogues, is the ritual blessing of the congregation by the kohanim (whose hands are ritually washed beforehand by the community's leviim) on holidays (and every morning in Israel).

But in spite of the fact that endogamous marriage for much of Diaspora history created an unusually high incidence of genetic linkage among Jews, Judaism has always accepted non-Jews into the fold through conversion. Abraham himself is referred to as the "first convert," and among famous Biblical personalities understood to have converted to Judaism are Jethro, the father-in-law of Moses, as well as Ruth, and several personalities from the rabbinic period, such as Shmaya and Avtalion. But even in the case of converts, the ideal of the Jews as a related family persists in the custom of converts taking a new, Jewish name upon their conversion. This name includes the patronymic used in all Jewish names—"ben" or "bat" so-and-so— but in the convert's case is "ben Abraham avinu v'Sara imeinu," (son—or daughter—of our father Abraham and our mother Sara). They are effectively adopted into the Abrahamic family. Today, children of a Jewish mother are recognized as Jewish in all groups and denominations. Even those movements (such as Reform) that have broadened their definition to also include those who have a Jewish father maintain a genetic conception of Jewish peoplehood (despite the fact that so-called "matrilineal descent" itself is a standard that seems to have emerged in the rabbinic period).

But for all the importance of unity and a common sense of historical descent that is understood to be a central feature of Jewish culture (for better and worse), in reality Jewish families and communities are quite diverse. The nature of the Jewish family has similarly (if not as radically) changed over time as well, and often in concert with developing gender relationships and roles in the non-Jewish communities among whom Jews lived. While it is impossible in a short book to describe the many different cultural and regional differences in ritual, this chapter will explore the historical evolution of the idea of the Jewish family and community, as well as gender roles and identities.

The Jewish Family

Jewish Marriage

The traditional image of the Jewish family is based in Biblical literature, especially the Torah. Given the age of these texts, we have precious little material that reflects the relationship between the texts and the lived, every-day reality of the Jewish family before the rabbinic period. Then, as with many areas of Jewish history, a significant material record emerged in the light of the rich archeological and literary sources from the Greco-Roman period. In Biblical literature, and later in Rabbinic literature, ideas of the family are thus preserved in two forms: narrative and legal.

The narrative descriptions of the ancient Israelite family form the basis of the later Jewish conception of family. The avot and imahot (forefathers and mothers), referring to Abraham and Sara's extended family, reflect an ideal model by which Jews have traditionally understood family, as do the very origins of humanity in the Bereshit creation story of Adam and Chava (Eve). In all cases, the Biblical idea of the Jewish family is patriarchal, with the male adult partner having extensive economic and legal authority over his wife and children. The Bible itself describes families as both monogamous and polygamous, with polygamous marriages playing an important part in the Torah's narrative: the case of Jacob, for instance, who was obliged to marry the daughters of his uncle Laban, Rachel and Leah, is a central early event in Israelite religious history. But in spite of its technical permissibility, polygamy was rare in Jewish practice through the ages, and was formally banned in the Ashkenazi world in the tenth century.

This codification of the legal ideal of the family emerges through myriad discussions in the Mishnah and Talmud. Like all Jewish law, of course, these categories—which cover nuptial and familial relations, including marriage contracts practices and rituals, permissible sexual partners and relations, divorce, means of detecting and punishing infidelity (always infidelity of the woman), levirate marriage (obligating marriage between a childless widow and the deceased husband's brother), among many other topics—originate in the written Torah itself. To this day, mastery of issues of family law is required as a basic qualification for an Orthodox rabbi.

Along with childbirth, marriage is the central event of adult Jewish life. Legal adulthood in Jewish law, and thus sexual relationships and standards for maturity and eligibility for marriage, was determined by the visible signs of puberty, and over time this age was settled at twelve for girls, and thirteen for boys. At this point, the child becomes a bar or bat mitzvah, a person obligated in observing the commandments. At the same time, there is no absolutely consistent trend of age of marriage; usually the social and economic status of the family dictated nuptial age, but ages seventeen to twenty-five would be considered normal in most historical contexts. As in most surrounding societies in which Jews lived, until the modern period the motivations for marriage were (and are) varied, including financial and emotional, usually depending upon the social status of the family. The idea of a "love match," or marriage as chosen by the bride and groom (chatan and kallah), while it likely existed in earlier periods of Jewish history in individual cases, was not an ideal until the nineteenth century, and then primarily only in the modernizing regions of Europe—similar to the majority population. At the same time, many marriages were likely a combination of a love match and an arranged marriage; often young couples, raised together in tight-knit communities, formed romantic bonds that were ratified by the permission of parents.

The idea of Jewish marriage itself is thoroughly legalistic. Its basic construction is a financial contract, which is still utilized nearly universally in Jewish weddings regardless of denomination to this day. This ketubah (marriage contract) utilizes, in traditional settings, the same Aramaic formula that evolved in the rabbinic period, which states the location of the wedding, the date, and technical expression of the nature of the financial exchange are described. The primary purpose of the ketubah is to specify the obligations of the groom to the bride. Over the course of the wedding ceremony, the bride is given the ketubah, it becomes "her" guarantee of the stipulations of the marriage—she possesses it as her property. In non-Orthodox settings, the text of the ketubah is either changed to reflect the sensibilities of the couple, or kept intact in its original form as a traditional symbol. Even in more liberal expressions of Orthodoxy some have extended the text of the ketubah to include provisions to protect the interests of the woman in the event that the marriage ends, compelling the husband to not delay in offering a divorce document (known as a get, see below).

The traditional ketubah understands gender relations in a transactional and patriarchal manner. Although it addresses the financial exchange on both sides of the partnership, it is the woman who is understood to be "sanctified"—that is, exclusively committed—to her husband through the marriage ceremony. Indeed, the only formal concept of marital infidelity in a traditional Jewish marriage is a married woman having prohibited sexual contact with another man, which has dire legal consequences. The most important of these is the status of mamzerut (illegitimacy), which bars the children of elicit sexual relations from any other marital partners except those of the same status. This understanding of gender roles fundamentally shapes the wedding ceremony itself. The specific rituals by which marriage was to be enacted are not described in detail in the Torah. Thus, like the ketubah, the core rituals of marriage in Judaism rose in the rabbinic period, and over time additional rituals were added, which vary regionally.

The wedding itself is divided into two parts: erusin (betrothal) and nisuin (formal marriage). Erusin (betrothal), also referred to as kidushin (sanctification), is the initial negotiation and agreement of the marriage, which involves rituals of formal financial exchange, obligating both parties (usually the bride's father and the groom or groom's father). For all intents and purposes, the couple is regarded as formally contracted to marriage and are accordingly restricted in their behavior with the opposite sex, to avoid inadvertent interactions that could nullify the agreement. In some situations, this concern could be quite serious, as the formal entrance into erusin effectively binds the woman in the eyes of halakha to her husband-to-be and could not be dissolved except through a formal divorce. For this reason, in contemporary practice erusin occurs immediately before the nisuin. Among the Orthodox, this is in accordance with the legally binding nature of the negotiation; in liberal denominations, when the custom is observed it is for symbolic reasons. The second part of the Jewish wedding is the nisuin (the marriage itself), also referred to as the chuppah (the term for the wedding canopy, after the most familiar accoutrement of the Jewish wedding). Legally, the nisuin is considered the formal completion of the marriage process, and its various elements symbolize the means by which the contract is enacted.

A traditional Jewish wedding today contains both the formal elements that initiate the marriage and embellishments based upon regionally specific cultural practices. Preceding the chuppah, the male members of both sides of the wedding party conclude the nisuin in a festive gathering, usually with celebratory drink and presentation of a dvar Torah, a "word of Torah," a short religious homily, delivered by the groom or another member of the party. There the formal, legal completion of the contract takes place. The ketubah document is read, a formal act of legal acquisition is performed (a general ceremony of legal acquisition, called kinyan), and two valid witnesses sign the ketubah to ratify the marriage. At the same time, the bride, in a separate location (usually another room in the same facility) is feted by the women of the wedding party and female guests, a counterpart to the nisuin called the haknasat kalla, a number of rituals intended to celebrate and welcome the bride to marriage.

Once the betrothal is concluded, the groom is escorted with singing and dancing to the seated bride, whose face he then covers with a veil after insuring that she is the intended bride. This ceremony is a reference to the Biblical story of the patriarch Jacob, whose intended bride Rachel was duplicitously exchanged without his knowledge for her sister, Leah, by their scheming father Laban. After this prologue, the wedding proceeds to the chuppah. The chuppah, or bridal canopy itself, is a symbolic dwelling place for the bride and groom. In the ancient period, it was likely a tent; from at least the medieval period forward, the chuppah has taken the form of a canopy, sometimes free-standing, but often held by honored guests as the ceremony is completed. It can be elaborately decorated and designed; it can just as often be a man's talit (prayer shawl) that is attached by each of its four corners to poles. The chuppah can take place in almost any location—among Ashkenazim, it was the practice to hold the chuppah outdoors, specifically to distinguish the Jewish wedding from the Christian practice of marriage in a church (in fact, some rabbinic authorities mandated this practice, although it is not universal).

The bride is then escorted to the chuppah, where the groom, witnesses, and a rabbi await. The rabbi serves in the role of the "mesader keddushin," (literally: overseer of the sanctification) who facilitates the correct procedure of the marriage ritual. The ceremony itself consists of several steps. First is recitation of the betrothal blessings over a first glass of wine by the officiant. Both the bride and groom then drink from the wine, and the groom then presents the bride with a ring, after presenting it to the witnesses to confirm that it is of appropriate value, reciting the formula: "You are consecrated to me with this ring according to the laws of Moses and Israel." The ring is then placed on the brides right hand index finger, again visibly to afford witnesses with a view that the act of exchange has been completed. A representative then reads the text of the ketubah. Finally, the officiant or an honored participant (or more than one), recites a series of blessings over a second cup of wine, which include sanctification of the occasion and wine, acknowledgment of God as creator of the commandment of gladdening the bride and groom, and a paeon to the anticipated return of the Jewish people to Israel.

At the conclusion of these blessings, referred to as the "sheva berachot" (seven blessings), in the final act—perhaps the most familiar ritual of the Jewish wedding—the groom breaks a glass. Although the most familiar version of this ritual is the groom stomping on the glass, Jews in different regions have adapted variant forms, such as throwing the glass or plate at a designated stone of the outside wall of the synagogue. The purpose of the ritual, based on an allusion in the Talmud, is to introduce a modicum of imperfection into the ceremony, in mourning for the unredeemed state of the Jewish people after the destruction of the Second Temple.

After the glass is crushed, the couple is escorted with fanfare by the wedding party to a private room, where a light meal has been laid out for them (in traditional circles, the bride and groom often fast the day of the wedding until after the ceremony). The couple is left alone, in theory for the first time, and the room carefully guarded by designated members of the wedding party to complete the custom of yichud (isolation). After a few minutes alone, the couple is escorted to the reception (usually), a festive occasion in which the entertainment of the bride and groom is regarded as an obligation upon all attending. At the conclusion of the wedding feast, the sheva berachot are again recited. For the following seven days, the bride and groom in a traditional context are feted by family and friends in festive meals where the sheva berachot are recited (a period referred to, not surprisingly, as the "sheva berachot").

Customs and laws of gender and sexuality

As a newly married bride, throughout Jewish history until the modern era (and up to the present day among Orthodox practitioners), a Jewish woman at marriage became obligated in the observance of the various commandments collectively referred to as taharat mishpachah (family purity). The term "tahara," from "tahor," meaning ritually pure, is a technical term whose most expansive use was in the requirements of ritual purity for priests conducting the Temple service. In the time when the Temple stood, the process of tahara (purification) after an encounter with a source of tumah (ritual impurity, most often a dead body or some article that came into contact with a body) required three elements: the passage of a requisite amount of time after the contamination, the offering of a sacrifice at the Temple at the end of the designated time, and immersion in the mikvah (ritual bath).

While it is now technically impossible for a Jewish person who has encountered tumah to regain ritual purity, the remaining forms of purification—time and immersion in the mikva—remain in place. One further residual custom regarding tumah and tahara is that of male kohanim to not knowingly expose themselves to tumah, for instance by being within a confined space (including a cemetery) with a dead body, the presumption being that they maintain some level of taharah. Finally, the mikvah was (and remains) the culmination of the ritual of conversion to Judaism (gerut): each new convert, after (if male) receiving circumcision (called hatafat dam brit) and examination by a bet din (a panel of three qualified persons, usually rabbis) of the convert's knowledge of Judaism and their earnestness as a convert, submerges in the mikvah and upon emerging is given their Jewish name and considered fully Jewish.

But the primary area where issues of ritual impurity and purification arise involves the status of a menstruating woman. At the onset of menses, a woman is considered by Jewish law to have entered a state of niddah (ritual impurity). A woman enters into this status with the appearance of blood from the vaginal area. Niddah status continues while the woman is menstruating, and upon its cessation for seven days. A woman is also considered a niddah after childbirth for a discrete period of time (seven days for a boy, fourteen for a girl). Upon the conclusion of niddah, that is, after a woman has examined herself and not seen discharge for seven days, she attends the mikvah following sunset and is no longer in niddah. Women do not go to the mikvah generally until marriage; indeed, one of the central traditional elements for a woman leading up to marriage is education in the obligations of taharat mishpachah, as well as her first visit to the mikvah before the ceremony itself.

There are significant implications of niddah for marital relations. A husband and wife are prohibited from sexual relations while a woman is in niddah. In strict Orthodox practice, this has led to many prohibitions of physical contact beyond simply refraining from sexual intercourse. While a woman is in niddah, she and her husband will sleep in separate beds, and will not serve food, drink, or pass objects directly to each other. Once the woman has passed seven "clean" days and has gone to the mikvah, she and her husband may resume marital relations and all other normal contact. This basic, monthly pattern of ritual behavior, without question, has an extensive impact on Jewish conceptions of gender and on gender relations.

Few outside Orthodox communities maintain the practice of taharat mishpacha. For the most part, this is because of a general decline in religious observance. Arcane, emotionally difficult, and, to modern sensibilities, ideologically suspect, observance of taharat mishpacha is also considered by rabbinic authorities to be an intensely personal issue. Although assessment of a woman's state of niddah ultimately is a halakhic decision, rabbis generally grant wide leeway in assuming compliance, and thus also even in Orthodox communities, levels of observance varies.

In liberal circles, to the extent that taharat mishpacha is even understood, its meaning has shifted with wider cultural currents. In the twentieth century, with the advent of greater women's empowerment and ultimately organized feminism, the core idea of taharat mishpacha and niddah status is problematic—the explicit origins of the practice in Torah and rabbinic literature are in the idea of a menstruating woman being ritually impure and taboo. Thus for most outside the Orthodox world, observance of the specifics of taharat mishpacha is nearly nonexistent. At the same time, some have embraced aspects of taharat mishpacha, especially the mikvah, recasting it as a symbol of women's empowerment and agency. There has thus been an increased attention to the dignity and quality of the mikvah and its importance as a sacred women's space.

In the last few decades, new conceptions of marriage and gender relations have become an increasingly visible issue in the Jewish world, as in many religious communities in increasingly tolerant and open societies. By and large, Jews affiliated with non-Orthodox streams of Judaism, as well as Israelis in general, tend to skew socially liberal and are generally supportive of greater acceptance of LGBTQ+ individuals, including, in the last few decades, sanctioning same-sex marriage and openly embracing non-heteronormative identities. The Reform movement in the United States has long taken up the cause of gender and sexual identity equality as part of a general activist turn in the 1960s and 1970s. It has formally allowed its rabbis to preside over same-sex marriages since 2000. This is consistent with its progressive attitude towards gender issues. The Reform movement also ordains women as rabbis, and has done so since the 1920s in Germany and the 1970s in the United States, by far the longest of any liberal Jewish movement. The Conservative movement has followed a more delayed trajectory, and until recently maintained that homosexual relations, same sex unions, and the ordination of openly LGBTQ+ clergy were impermissible. However, in recent decades, in step with wider social and cultural acceptance, it has softened its position considerably, and presently

Conservative rabbis are permitted to officiate at gay marriage ceremonies, be openly gay and in the clergy, while stopping short of fully legitimating all LGBTQ+ identities and behavior.

In Orthodox communities, due to the observance of halakha as an immutable cornerstone of religious identity, alternative sexual and gender identity is far more fraught, but in practice not inflexible. The primary prohibition regarding homosexuality in halakhically-organized Judaism is that the Torah explicitly forbids male-on-male penetrative sex (as the prohibition is generally understood). Over eons, this has predictably been interpreted widely to include behaviors that violate socially heteronormative gender relations, as worldwide, Jewish communities were almost entirely located within Christian and Muslim societies, both of which have condemnatory attitudes towards homosexuality. At the same time, gender and marriage relationships common in majority cultures are not necessarily replicated in a subaltern community such as Diaspora Jewry. Thus, when the question of later conceptions of gender and sexual identity began to take on significant social force at the end of the twentieth century, unlike in conservative Christianity and Islam, Judaism had no obvious dogmatic position. Most in the Orthodox camp maintain that the Torah's condemnation of a specific sexual act equals a blanket prohibition on all non-heteronormative identities and behaviors. However, a minority of Orthodox rabbinic figures have taken more nuanced positions, varying from outright acceptance of gay relationships to muted neutrality or tolerance.

Finally, transgender identity, which has become more open and common generally in Israel, the US and Europe, has similarly required the Orthodox to grapple with questions of identity not clearly adjudicated in halakha. Interestingly, perhaps because transgender identity has no necessary relationship to sexual activity, transgender Jews in the Orthodox community may in some instances experience less resistance than cisgendered, gay Orthodox Jews. In several instances, rabbis even in more conservative Orthodox circles have found halakhic grounds for tolerance and inclusion of transgender Orthodox individuals.

Divorce in Judaism

As with its initiation, the dissolution of marriage in Jewish tradition is a legal process. Unlike Christianity, Judaism has a pragmatic attitude towards divorce. Like any legal contract, a marriage can be dissolved for failure to fulfill the terms of the contract. In halakhic literature, there are numerous grounds for the granting of a divorce (the Hebrew term is a get, after the document that codifies the divorce). Either partner traditionally may divorce the other if the marriage is childless; a woman may divorce her husband for a broad range of mistreatments. Functionally, a divorce is enacted when the husband grants a get, either based on his own belief that the marriage should be ended (for specific causes which are enumerated in the halakhic literature) or his wife's demand. If it is determined that the husband is liable for the dissolution, he is required to provide the support stipulated in the ketubah, and vice-versa. It is the husband who must grant the get, physically placing it in her hand in a ceremony overseen by a beit din of three qualified individuals (including the rabbi who writes the get on parchment) in order to effect the divorce.

While in the majority of Jewish divorces the husband fulfills the obligation to grant a get, in some non-amicable divorces, a husband may refuse to grant the get to the wife, leaving her in an untenable situation of being prohibited from remarrying (as she is still considered obligated to her husband). Due to the basic inequity in the halakhic conception of marriage—that the wife is consecrated *to* the husband, while he has no parallel status—a woman seeking divorce has little recourse in the eyes of halakha. In the present day, this "agunah problem" (agunah, or "chained woman," is a woman who cannot remarry because she is regarded as still married to an absent husband)— is a unique social issue in the Orthodox world. For the most part, it falls to the community to enforce compliance through socially and ritually shunning a husband who withholds a get maliciously, and a number of social activist organizations exist today to combat the problem of agunot. So concerning is this issue to the Orthodox community that in the most liberal wings of Orthodoxy, even the ketubah itself has been adapted to include a clause that requires the husband to grant a get if demanded. This clause is controversial, however, and is not employed outside of the modern Orthodox community.

Childbirth and Early Childhood

Children and Childbirth in Jewish Culture

The birth of children in the Jewish world is, not surprisingly, a central, sacred event in the family and community. In religious terms, propagation is regarded as a specific commandment derived from the text of Bereshit, "pru u'rvu" (be fruitful and multiply), and Jewish law interprets this phrase as a mandate that a married couple attempt to have at least one child of each gender. Historically, attitudes towards childbirth and child rearing have been influenced by internal customs and attitudes and the norms of external society, as with other areas of Jewish family life.

In the early modern (pre-nineteenth century) world, high rates of infant mortality had a profound impact on attitudes towards childbirth. Although a tight-knit, fairly closed religious group, Jews were nevertheless affected by the same low standards of medical knowledge and the identification of sexual activity with procreation, and thus frequent pregnancy, childbirth and child-rearing was the lot and primary occupation of most Jewish women. The focus on childbirth and Jewish rituals around pregnancy reflect the long history of its being one of the most dangerous health conditions faced by a woman in the pre-modern period. Numerous customs and superstitions—such as not announcing a pregnancy openly, not naming a child until after birth (or after circumcision, for a boy)—are residual reminders of belief that open discussion of a future Jewish life would attract malignant supernatural powers. Indeed, a fair amount of practical Jewish mysticism is less concerned with the ontological questions of theoretical kabbalah than with providing protections, in the form of amulets and other magical formulae, for pregnant women and women in childbirth.

In contemporary Jewish societies, attitudes towards childbirth follow a similar pattern to other aspects of Jewish life: the more religiously conservative, the more practices are retained from earlier periods. This includes birthrates. In non-

Orthodox families, rates of childbirth are lower and in line with general, secular individuals and communities. In Orthodox communities, on the other hand, where childbirth is considered a divine obligation, birthrates tend to be much higher. In addition to the commandment of "pru u'rvu," Orthodox Jews also view themselves as having a further divine obligation, not codified in halakha, to "replace" the numbers of the victims of the Holocaust, as an important element of contemporary Orthodox identity it is a (not inaccurate) sense of unique victimization by the crimes of the Holocaust.

Brit Milah

Eight days after the birth of a boy, he is brought into the covenant of the Jewish people through the circumcision ritual, brit milah. This is the infant boy's first encounter with Jewish law and custom, and is the most foundational ritual in Jewish religious practice and history. Its origins as a divine commandment reach back to Abraham, who is described in the Torah as being commanded by God to remove his foreskin and those of all the males in his household to mark the covenant between God and the Jewish people.

Significance of Brit Milah

The ritual of Brit Milah is so deeply embedded in the customs, history and religious belief of the Jewish people as to be nearly synonymous with being a Jewish male. Underscoring this is the ubiquity of circumcision among Jews to this day. Although in the modern period there have been occasional attempts to limit or abandon the practice among those who argue it is offensive to modern sensibilities and of dubious medical or hygienic value, they usually do not identify religiously with any specific denomination.

The obligation to perform the circumcision ceremony falls upon the father, who in most cases appoints a proxy, a mohel (trained circumciser), due to the delicacy and technical requirements of the task. While it is not necessary that a mohel be a rabbi, in contemporary practice, he most often is. As the ceremony begins, a person of honor, referred to as the sandek (godfather, approximately), is seated in a chair designated the "kisei Eliyahu" (throne of Elijah) with a pillow on his lap. The baby is brought into the room (often circumcisions are held in the synagogue, as the circumcision should optimally occur immediately after the morning prayer service, but it is not necessary) and placed on the pillow. The person who actually performs the act, the father or mohel, is responsible for reciting the blessing over the act, "blessed is God, Sovereign of the Universe, who has sanctified us with his commandments and commanded us concerning circumcision." The father (if the father is not the mohel) then recites a second blessing, "...who has commanded us to enter him [the child] into the covenant of Abraham." As he does so, the mohel then utilizes a purpose-built clamp and scalpel to sever the foreskin of the infant's penis, and then performs a required extraction of a drop of blood to confirm the completion of the ritual. The baby's wound is covered, the baby is lifted and the mohel is then given a glass of wine, over which he recites the blessing for wine as well as the naming of the child, dips a finger into the wine and places a minute amount into the child's mouth. The ceremony thus concluded, the congregation present, as in all other smachot (religious celebrations), a festive meal is consumed and the birkat hamazon (blessing after the meal) is recited, with special additions in honor of the brit milah.

Before the twentieth century, there was no comparable ceremony for a newborn girl in Ashkenazi communities. When a girl was born, she was named in the synagogue when the father received an aliyah to the Torah in the first scheduled Torah reading after the birth. In the Sephardi world there is the custom of Zeved ha-bat (gift of the daughter), in which a festive meal accompanies the announcement and naming of the girl in synagogue. In recent decades, a naming ceremony for girls has become widely practiced outside the Orthodox world, and increasingly the non-Sephardi Orthodox world has adapted similar practices in the form of the Simchat bat. Generally speaking, there is less acceptance of this custom in more conservative Orthodox quarters.

Inside the Jewish Home

Jewish homes have developed for centuries in response to the dynamic of internal Jewish ritual and legal requirements, and external interaction with surrounding societies. The common characteristic shared by all Jewish cultures is the intertwining of religious obligation and embrace of customs outside of the tradition.

Food and the Jewish Household

Perhaps the most vivid area dynamics of domestic culture in Jewish history is in the world of food. As a fundamental domestic activity as well as the organization of the pre-modern household (every Jewish home, like non-Jewish homes in the pre-modern period, was organized around the hearth as the center of cooking, warmth, and family socialization), cuisine and its accoutrements are among the better-preserved artifacts and represent a copious source of information about daily life.

Like most other areas of life, cuisine in traditional Jewish culture is governed by halakha. The basic requirements of kashrut (dietary laws) are stated in numerous places in the Torah, and center around three concerns: foods that are restricted or permitted based upon their "cleanliness," or ritual fitness; foods that may or may not be consumed together, primarily meat and dairy products; and finally the means of slaughter which render an animal fit for consumption. The Torah contains a detailed list of what animals, fowl, fish and insects are permitted. For the most part, among mammals and fowl these correspond to animals that are considered ritually fit, that is, suitable for sacrifice on the altar. This includes herbivore ruminants, both domestic and wild (cattle, sheep, goats, deer), and fowl (predatory birds and scavengers are considered unfit). The Torah offers a dual test for what qualifies a mammal as kosher: it must chew a cud and have split hooves, which excludes some domestic animals (horses, pigs) and predatory mammals. Although there is no stated logic in the Torah, fish are also subjected to a two-part standard: fish that do not have both scales and fins (which excludes primarily cartilaginous fish and shellfish) are not considered kosher.

Further paralleling the relationship between permitted foods (especially fowl and meat) and Temple ritual is the requirement for kosher slaughter. While all of the laws of kashrut, including shechita (ritual slaughter), are indicated in the Torah, as in other areas, it is in the halakhic literature that the specific practice is explained. Because of its central importance to Jewish life, knowledge of the rules of kosher food preparation is a basic area of competence required for rabbis, which remains the case for Orthodox rabbis today, whom must demonstrate proficiency in the laws of kashrut to receive their ordination. All kosher mammals and birds must be ritually slaughtered in a means that parallels the practices of slaughter in the Temple to be considered permissible for consumption. First, they must be slaughtered by a trained individual, someone who has established their ability to perform the slaughter efficiently and without error. The shochet (ritual slaughterer) makes a blessing on the mitzvah of shechita, then uses a highly sharpened and polished blade to sever the majority of the trachea and esophagus of the animal in a continuous cutting motion, without pausing. The blood is allowed to spill as much as possible (full exsanguination of the animal is a requirement of kashrut), and then the blood is covered with dirt (another commandment that is accompanied with a blessing). After the animal is butchered, the meat must then be soaked in salt brine to extract remaining blood from the tissue, at which point the meat is kosher for consumption. The specific requirements of the slaughter, butchery and exsanguination of the animal are numerous and specific, and any error—especially in the slaughter itself—renders the animal unfit for consumption, although its meat can be sold to a non-Jewish consumer.

The final area of restriction in kosher consumption of food revolves around a specific commandment of the Torah: that Jews not eat a "kid boiled in its mother's milk." This strange construction in the Torah, offered without an explicit rationale, was interpreted in the rabbinic period to restrict consumption of milk and meat together in one sitting. While the technical meaning literally suggests that one must eat milk and meat separately, in practice it is an expansive prohibition. In rabbinic interpretation, it means that one may not cook milk and meat together (or even use the same utensils), eat milk and meat at the same time (the period of separation between consumption of milk and meat varies depending on community, generally from one to six hours), nor even consume milk and meat on the same dishes. Thus, in contemporary Orthodox and traditional Jewish homes (including many homes in non-Orthodox families and individuals that observe kashrut), families maintain two sets of dishes, milk and meat, and another two sets of dishes for Pesach, where restrictions on the consumption of leavened wheat demand a higher level of kashrut for the holiday.

Education

In pre-modern Jewish society, where Jews had a significant amount of communal autonomy as a tolerated minority in predominantly monarchic or aristocratic societies, childhood both shared basic similarities with surrounding cultures and differed sharply from it. For young Jewish boys, unlike most surrounding premodern cultures in which Jews dwelt, education was a central cultural value. The obligation to instruct one's sons in Torah is an explicit commandment, but before the modern period, education for girls was regarded as one of the domestic tasks of the mother (with rare exceptions). Boys on the other hand began their Torah education at as young as three to five years old, at which point they entered into formal education, most commonly a primary school referred to in Ashkenaz as the heder and in the Sephardi and Mizrahi world as the talmud torah.

These schools were often poorly organized and maintained, sometimes supported by the community, more often privately through payment of tuition, usually meeting in the residence of the melamed (elementary teacher). Organized institutional communal primary education more familiar to modern eyes did not begin in earnest in Ashkenazi communities until the nineteenth century, and in Sephardi and Mizrahi communities, the mid-nineteenth century and later. The traditional curriculum was prioritized accomplishing competency in basic Jewish texts, such as the siddur and the Torah with its most prominent commentaries (especially Rashi). Around ages seven or eight, boys would typically begin studying more complex rabbinic texts, especially Mishnah and, eventually, Talmud.

As boys progressed in their education, there was little structure to the curriculum, and more textually-dexterous students moved at a faster pace. Depending on the economic level of the family or the community, boys tended to study until the age of around thirteen, when they either moved forward into an advanced academy, called a yeshiva, or began learning a trade. Those who were able to attend yeshiva usually did so because of familial affluence (the ability to afford supporting the child was central), because the level of the boy's textual abilities earned him independent or communal financial support to continue his studies, or both.

Before the early nineteenth century, the yeshiva was a local affair. The rabbi of a community would almost always have his own beyt midrash (study hall), and depending on his caliber and reputation, might attract students both locally and from abroad. More prestigious rabbinic figures often drew a significant number of students from distant locations. For young men who ascended to study in yeshiva, there was not necessarily an expectation that they proceed further to clerical careers, although it is from these ranks that rabbis emerged. In wealthier families it was common for young men to be sponsored in their studies by their parents to improve their marriage prospects. Promising Torah scholars were often sought-after for marriage by wealthy parents, and it was common for part of the marriage negotiations in such cases to include a number of years of financial support for the young man to continue full-time study.

At the end of the eighteenth century, especially in central and western Europe, the traditional educational model which had persisted for centuries began to collapse together with other elements of the autonomous Jewish community. Coinciding with rapid political and social change culminating in the French Revolution, European kingdoms increasingly sought to centralize power and rationalize governance. Consistently, Gentile governments viewed Jewish communal structure and autonomy as detrimental to their centralizing projects, and sought ways to integrate Jews into the larger body politic. The reform of Jewish education was a primary tactic. It became the most common thread in European legislation affecting Jews from the mid-eighteenth century through the middle of the nineteenth. In several states, policy focused on Jewish education, along with Jewish occupations and industry, as the levers to transform the Jewish community from its traditional status into fuller (or at least more economically productive) participation with the state. In each of the central-east European empires, decrees were issued which demanded Jews enter into non-Jewish educational institutions, or mandated governmental oversight of Jewish schools and yeshivas.

The result of this over the long term was a dramatic transformation of Jewish education. Beginning early in western countries such as France, Jews took with alacrity to the opportunity of entering into non-Jewish schools, and education indeed became an ideal route to integration and assimilation. In central and eastern Europe, the issue was more contentious. In Prussia and other German territories, Jews transitioned fairly quickly to sending children —boys and girls—to non-Jewish schools, including university, once they were an option. In other instances, Jewish communities established their own Jewish schools in concert with governmental oversight and regulation. Still, there was outspoken resistance to this process by traditionalist rabbis (who increasingly identified themselves as "Orthodox") who regarded this process—correctly—as an attempt to displace a central cornerstone of Jewish culture and identity with one oriented towards a non-Jewish culture and society. In response, some German Orthodox leaders, such as Samson Raphael Hirsch, sought a compromise: to create a private Jewish school system, supported by the private donations and tuition of parents in the community, which combined intensive Torah study along the lines of the traditional yeshiva with a modern secular education. While this model had limited success in Europe, it would become the central model in the United States in the late twentieth century, re-constituted as the idea of the Jewish day school.

Another important part of this general modernization of Jewish education effected a significant change in attitudes towards girls' education. By the end of the nineteenth century, girls on all points of the ideological spectrum attended school formally, usually state schools. Finally, even the most conservative Orthodox, those most resistant to modernization (women's education was regarded as a modern innovation in conservative Orthodox circles) endorsed a women's school system, Beis Yaakov, which tacitly underscored a broad consensus that education for women was an essential part of Jewish communal values across the ideological spectrum.

In eastern Europe (in this case, the Russian Empire), a more heavy-handed approach to ending Jewish autonomy and isolation led to a more resistant attitude toward reforming Jewish education. Already at a disadvantage given the much larger, much more entrenched Jewish communities than those in western and central Europe, the autocratic Russian government viewed Jews with deep suspicion, and were reluctant to extend rights (although this was essentially the same attitudes held towards the general Russian population), and imposed draconian regulations on an overwhelmingly traditional and unreceptive Jewish population. Thus, in the Russian Empire, Jewish education took an alternative path of modernization in the form of a reconceptualized model of the yeshiva. Beginning with the Volozhin yeshiva in 1803, this model remade the yeshiva into a full-time, advanced academic academy of Talmudic study, with an ideal of preventing Jewish youth from engaging in government-sponsored alternatives. The modern yeshiva kept the traditional content of the older model, but adapted modern innovations such as a fixed curriculum, a faculty of rabbinic teachers, and a more or less standardized policy of acceptance, in place of the traditional, local yeshivot that preceded it.

In the Ottoman empire, which contained the largest Jewish population outside of Europe, government reforms and modernization, collectively referred to as the "Tanzimat" reforms from the late 1830s through the turn of the twentieth century, did not reach as far into the practices of Jewish communities. Although a re-definition of Jewish status in relation to the majority Islamic society and government was part of these reforms, Jews in the Ottoman Empire retained extensive communal autonomy as a protected (dhimmi) religious minority group. As a theocratic government, even if a modernizing one, the Ottomans were slow to change a social structure mandated by Sharia (the body of Islamic law). Within these communities, the traditional talmud torah remained unquestionably the central pillar of Jewish education, as did the advanced yeshivot.

The primary challenge to this traditional model came not from the Ottoman government, but as a result of European (especially French) colonial interests in North Africa and the Middle East. Following in the footsteps of French cultural evangelism in the Middle East, prominent members of the French Jewish community (which, by the mid-nineteenth century, was deeply integrated into French culture) created the Alliance Israelite Universelle, a philanthropic organization with a mission to create a modern, French-style education system among North African and Middle Eastern Jewish communities, tasked with imparting European values and modern skills to what they regarded as a primitive and exploited Jewish community. The Alliance school system established schools throughout North Africa and the Levant, attracted a number of students, and was seen as real competition for the local talmud torah system. It was a major force of modernization—and European cultural identification—for Jews in the Islamic world.

By the mid twentieth century, significant social and cultural change had utterly re-cast the nature of Jewish education and the choices Jews had for educating their children. The United States, which by mid-century possessed the largest Jewish population in the world, overwhelmingly chose to take advantage of the secular, publicly-funded education system that burgeoned in the progressive era. Beyond availability and affordability, this choice offered Jewish immigrants something that they had been largely denied in their countries of origin: a straightforward path to integration into the majority culture. This was not viewed as uniformly positive across the Jewish world. Nevertheless, between the onset of mass Jewish immigration from Russia in the early 1880s through the 1920s and beyond, thousands upon thousands of Jewish parents chose to place their children on the path of Americanization through public schooling.

This represented a massive shift in cultural values: These immigrants had come primarily from traditionally-oriented, religiously conservative and highly isolated Jewish communities in the Russian Empire. Although there were secular educational opportunities for Jews offered by the state, they were viewed largely with suspicion and utilized by only a minority. Now, disembarking in the new world with a relatively open society, a rapid shift by many to an American identity took place, which was facilitated by the presence of a significant number of options for how they could identify with Judaism. Unlike in Russia, the Reform movement in the United States was robust and powerful, leading by miles perception of Judaism in the public sphere. In these decades, Jews began to see public acceptance and participation in civic life that had never quite been equaled in their historical experience, and this also contributed to a strong sense of identification with American identity and a rapid, largely successful

integration into American society. To the present
day, the overwhelming majority of Jews in America
utilize the same education system as non-Jews
and identify strongly with American culture. At
the same time, this now near-complete process of
integration has caused, and continues to cause, a
great deal of existential tension in the American
Jewish community: a fear that Jewish identity is
being lost entirely.

One answer to this has been the continuation
—albeit with modern, American adjustments—
of parochial Jewish education in lieu of American
non-Jewish options. In the Orthodox community,
parochial education has become nearly universal.
Orthodox schools, referred to as either Jewish
day schools or yeshivas, run a spectrum ranging
from modern, progressive secular education with
traditional Torah study to fully traditional, east
European-style yeshivas. Depending on the flavor
of Orthodoxy to which the school adheres, they may
include as much secular education as a modern,
secular primary or secondary school, or as little
secular material as American law allows. In areas
where there is a high concentration of Hasidic or non-
Hasidic conservative Orthodox communities, often
members of the community will run for election in
municipal governments and school boards to ensure
community control over how much, and how, secular
studies are instructed in Jewish schools. In most
Jewish schools in America, English is the language of

instruction; in more insular communities, Yiddish is the primary language in some schools.

Outside of the Orthodox world in America, non-Orthodox Jews have also created parochial educational institutions, but they are far smaller, less-integrated and generally less attractive to American Jews, who are less concerned with the lack of an intensive, full-time Jewish communal educational experience. These institutions have a more modest component of religious studies, a much larger focus on fostering Jewish cultural identity and positive identification with the State of Israel. Finally, in some areas, independent "community" Jewish schools, with no overt denominational orientation, provide private Jewish education for a relatively small minority of American Jews.

Another important avenue of fostering a robust Jewish identity is the large network of Jewish summer camps in North America. Like Jewish primary and secondary schools, the Jewish camp system emerged out of the need for burgeoning early twentieth century Jewish communities to create parallel institutions to those (such as northeastern summer camps) from which they were excluded or which were otherwise not an option. Over the twentieth century and up to the present day, the summer camps that dot the mountainous regions of Pennsylvania and upstate New York (as well as their descendants across the country) have formed a central part in the collective cultural identity of

American Jews across all expressions of Judaism, from the most conservative Hasidic to the entirely non-religious, even secular political movements of the American Jewish community.

On the other side of the Atlantic, Jews in Israel replicate some of the American patterns. There, too, the majority of Jewish Israeli children are educated in secular, public Israeli schools, which are comparable to other such institutions elsewhere. At the same time, as Israel maintains a commitment to supporting the Jewish culture of the state, public schools run a full gamut from fully secular to modern Orthodox institutions. Among the more insular, conservative Orthodox—the massive Hasidic and non-Hasidic Haredi communities that are a powerful force in Israeli politics and society—these communities' considerable growth and youth have led to the creation of a prodigious system of traditional primary schools and yeshivot. These institutions, even more perhaps than their American counterparts, have full control over their curricula and the culture of their institutions. Although the heder-yeshiva system is most identified with Ashkenazi culture, even among Haredi Sephardi and Mizrahi communities in Israel this model has become the dominant one in Haredi education.

As with primary and secondary school, Jewish engagement with higher education has also evolved over the last century. From early in modern European Jewish history, a small number of Jews attended

European universities (in some places as early as the seventeenth century) in which, for the most part, they were relegated to a few specific fields (predominantly medicine). Until the nineteenth century, however, the overwhelming majority of Jews (meaning, in this case, Jewish boys) were educated in the traditional setting as described above. As with many other facets of modernization, a dramatic change in this occurred in the first few decades of the nineteenth century, as modernizing and centralizing European states began widening (and actively encouraging) educational opportunities for Jews, which included expanding access to university. Somewhat later, Jews in the Russian Empire were also given access to university education, although only a minority had actually ventured far enough into Russian non-Jewish education to be able to qualify for entrance, either through attendance at a Russian school or through their own autodidactic efforts.

By the twentieth century, university attendance for Jews in western and central Europe and the United States, while not universal, frequently outstripped surrounding ethnicities. In some major European universities, such as Vienna, Jewish university attendance was often a point of contention, as in some cases above twenty percent of the university population could, at a given time, be Jewish (out of a much smaller percentage of the general population) and could go above thirty percent (as in Vienna in the fin de siecle period). The situation was similar in the

United States; although it was not until mid-century that college education became a staple of middle class American identity, Jews—many of them immigrants or their first generation descendants—viewed university education as a further enhancement of their economic prospects and their Americanization. As a result, Jews also attended college at higher rates than comparable, non-Jewish socioeconomic groups. In both Europe and the United States, this perceived Jewish "domination" of university population was periodically a pretext for anti-Semitism, and often the non-Jewish student population—especially in central Europe—represented the cutting edge of anti-Semitic agitation. Occasionally, states and universities used bureaucratic mechanisms (such as quotas and numerus clausus) to restrict Jewish enrollment. In the United States, these restrictions in the early twentieth century were motivation for the establishment of Jewish institutions of higher education—most notably the modern Orthodox Yeshiva University in New York City, which would grow to include multiple undergraduate colleges and advanced faculties in Judaic studies, medicine, law, business, and mental health. Brandeis University in the suburbs of Boston, which has no parochial affiliation, offers much the same, as does the American Jewish University in Los Angeles, and other small Hebrew colleges in Philadelphia and Boston. While no parochial university comparable to Yeshiva University was established by non-Orthodox denominations, both the Conservative and Reform movements established their own theological seminaries in the nineteenth century that continue to operate to this day as the intellectual centers of the movement. Finally, in Israel the university system, modelled after the European university model, which includes The Hebrew University of Jerusalem, the Technion, Ben Gurion University and Bar Ilan University, among others, have emerged as internationally prestigious institutions of higher education.

In the more conservative Orthodox world, the educational model of the yeshiva system reigns supreme, but it too has evolved over the twentieth century. The remnant of the great yeshivas in Europe that were destroyed in the Holocaust and their communities moved to the United States and Israel (although others relocated to places such as Manchester, United Kingdom, the location of an important yeshiva to this day). While these institutions were initially small and insular, over the course of the twentieth century they have grown significantly along with the considerable demographic growth. Major institutions such as the Beyt Medresh Govoha (the Lakewood Yeshiva in suburban New Jersey) are themselves the size of universities, with the infrastructure of small towns. At the same time, affluence and a reification of the ideal of the Jewish male spending all his time learning Torah have created a renaissance of religious learning, while at the same time exacerbating certain social problems, especially communal poverty. In Israel, where exemption from military service (which is not condoned by many conservative Orthodox authorities) offers a decided incentive, young men will often remain in yeshiva or kollel (for married students) well into their adult lives.

Patterns of Jewish Adulthood and Occupations

In contemporary times, most Jews are almost entirely integrated into the general culture of the places they live. Almost all of the vestiges of Jewish difference externally—dress, language, social groups, occupations—have all disappeared outside of the most insular Orthodox communities (which have maintained these markers, most obviously dress and language, for ideological reasons). Nevertheless, aspects of the historical experience of isolation, social and cultural exclusion, and persecution have left a mark on contemporary life and occupational choices.

Historically Jews were often discriminated against as a collective, and were excluded from many areas of economic life and social interaction with non-Jews. In part this was punitive and based upon anti-Jewish attitudes, and in part it reflected an internal Jewish desire to keep separate from non-Jews. By the nineteenth century, modernizing European states intervened extensively in Jewish communal affairs to both entice and coerce Jews into integration. By the end of the century, this process had succeeded in dramatically shrinking the traditional centers of power in the Jewish community. In many places, the community was abolished altogether, or restructured into a modern bureaucracy with little power over the daily lives of its members.

Interestingly, many of the components of Jewish economic life in earlier periods played an important role in Jewish integration into modern society. For most of their history in the medieval and early modern periods, Jews were a minority that tended to live in more densely populated settings, oriented towards activities of commerce, trade and the other few occupations that were open to them. Excluded in most cases from owning land, Jews rarely were engaged in agricultural occupations. Finally, as discussed above, for a long stretch of European history, Jews placed more emphasis on the importance of education and literacy than their host societies, which grew directly out of the deeply-held value of Torah study in traditional society.

All of these tendencies played a role in the evolution of modern Jewish adulthood and occupations. In most cultures into which Jews began to integrate in the nineteenth century, the route to family and communal economic security, engagement and, hopefully, acceptance in general society was through putting these culturally- and historically-derived attributes to work. In addition to Jews embracing broadening educational opportunities, they were well-positioned to move into a relatively new form of economic life: the white-collar occupation. Especially in rapidly modernizing states such as the Austrian Empire, Germany, France, and the United States, but even in more slowly-modernizing states such as Russia and the Ottoman Empire, Jews were consistently among the vanguard of a new, rising urban middle class. Simply put, Jews were well-situated to enjoy the fruits of modernization.

Within a short period of time, Jews in central Europe in the nineteenth century, one of the most rapidly-modernizing regions in the world, went from traditionalist occupations to modern middle-class, private-sector occupations. Many of the mid-level managers and employees of the growing professionalization of all aspects of economic life had grandfathers who had sold small goods door-to-door as peddlers. The ranks of lawyers, the specialists in the expanding regulatory and bureaucratic structure of the nineteenth century European state, were supplemented by young men whose fathers had known only the heder of the Polish shtetl. Medicine, which was one of the earliest occupations open to Jews that required an elite education (Jews were being trained in some European universities in medicine since the seventeenth century), remained an especially popular field, and the growth of science and professionalization of medicine counted on the contributions of many Jews for this reason. Even in communal occupations—rabbis and other functionaries—modernization and professionalization became the norm. Communities increasingly sought rabbis with a modern education, and the ability to serve as a pastoral leader and homilist replaced the older view that the only rabbinic skill that really mattered was his accomplishment in Torah learning and acumen in legal reasoning.

By the turn of the twentieth century, these trends had created substantial inequality between Jewish populations based upon geography.

Synagogues, Culture, and Jewish Modernization

For Jews who lived in states that had aggressively modernized, there was an almost universal embrace of social and economic integration and a generally higher level of affluence. Even Jewish culture in its religious forms and its material production reflected this. The synagogue service and its physical appearance and layout began to borrow extensively from the tastes of the surrounding culture. Several examples of the grand synagogues of the German-speaking Jewish world, still standing from present-day Poland to San Francisco, attest to the tight Jewish embrace of nineteenth century bourgeois culture.

In areas where modernization moved more slowly, such as Russia and the Ottoman Empire, Jewish communities remained far more traditional, insular, and resistant to social or cultural engagement with non-Jewish society. While engagement did occur, it tended to be in precisely those areas where new opportunities were opened up because of attempts at modernization. In the Russian Empire, for example, the judicial reforms of Alexander II in the early 1860s created a demand for a judicial bureaucracy, and especially attorneys, which became an important avenue of integration for some Russian Jews. Similarly, Russia's steps towards a modern market economy, which had a devastating effect on traditional Jewish occupations in the Pale of Settlement, led to significant movement of Jews into Russian cities (such as Odessa) and towards modern urban occupations.

All of these trends accelerated in the twentieth century. Central European Jewry, now well-represented on both sides of the Atlantic, had integrated into general culture for the most part. As for Russian Jewry, intensifying persecution in the late Russian Empire led to some three million Jews leaving the country in a little over four decades, most immigrating to the United States. Here, most rapidly acculturated and modernized, sometimes within a single generation. Not long after the beginning of this mass migration, Russia itself was shaken by convulsive revolutions, and after 1917 integrating Jews into the new Soviet society became one priority of the Bolsheviks. Religious culture was discouraged, undermined, and ultimately persecuted. Though vestiges of anti-Jewish stigma still persisted after the end of the Tsarist regime, for instance in the retention of "Jewish" as a nationality, it was expected that Soviet Jews would finally shed their particularism and integrate fully into the Soviet system. Thus, although the Soviet Union would experience periodic outbursts of anti-Semitism, by the mid-twentieth century there was little to distinguish Jewish Soviet citizens from non-Jews. As in the United States, Jews rose in Soviet society to all levels of social and occupational positions.

Today, Jewish daily life the world over, including all but the most insular Orthodox communities, is mostly indistinguishable from non-Jewish daily life. In the United States and Europe, the remaining Diaspora communities still largely reflect the levels of social accomplishment, cultural integration and affluence that grew out of their early adaptation of the trappings of the modern middle class. This is also the case with economic life: Jews in most Diaspora communities cluster in their occupations to fields that skew towards higher levels of education (doctors, academics, lawyers) and other white-collar professions. This is the case regardless of levels of cultural integration.

Even in the most conservative Orthodox groups, although a life dedicated to Torah study is the cultural ideal, highly-educated professionals in medicine, law, academia and other fields from among Hasidic and other deeply traditionalist communities is not uncommon for either men or women. At the same time, depending on the intensity of traditionalism or, at the other extreme, laxity of connection to the Jewish community, the result has been more diversity of occupations at both extremes. Jews who did not grow up with tight connections to any Jewish community tend to reflect the general occupations and socioeconomic patterns of non-Jews. Conversely, in intensely insular Orthodox communities, communal self-sufficiency and prioritizing economic support of group members has led Jews to adopt any number of historically untraditional professions and occupations.

Employment and occupation patterns in the other major world Jewish population—the Jews of Israel—follows this pattern. In part, this is due to an attitude present in Zionism from its inception in the late nineteenth century (see Chapter 3). As early Jewish nationalists theorized the cause of the many social ills faced by the Jewish population in Europe, a consistent theme was a collective self-criticism: that Jews, by virtue of their exclusion and persecution, had been forced into "unnatural" and unhealthy occupations that had tainted the Jewish character and amplified the criticisms of anti-Semites. Thus a central cultural ethos of Israeli attitudes towards Jewish work and occupation was that a return to "productive" labor—which early Zionists associated with agricultural and industrial labor—would both build the state and reform the Diaspora "mentality" that plagued the Jewish people and contributed to their oppression. At the same time, as the idea of a modern nation-state of Israel gained more currency and reality, an important consensus on the desirability of an *exclusively* Jewish labor force in the nascent state emerged in response to increasing tension with Palestinian Arab labor. Indeed, by the time of the Israeli war for independence, the yishuv (the Jewish community of the land of Israel) had become mostly self-sufficient. The implications of this history for modern patterns of occupation and employment in Israel are significant. In Israel today, Jews do indeed engage in every conceivable occupation in society, are restricted from none, and have made considerable innovations in areas—such as agriculture and manufacturing—that would have been inconceivable in the Diaspora model.

Death in Jewish Culture

The last of the life-cycle events in the Jewish world is, not surprisingly, death. As with the rituals of birth—especially circumcision—the ancient rituals surrounding death in the Jewish world are observed by a majority of Jews, including those outside the Orthodox fold. And, as with most contemporary Jewish ritual, they are based upon Biblical sources, processed and ritualized by the rabbis of the Talmud and passed down, largely intact, in their current form. While some individuals and communities in more progressive circles may circumscribe or re-interpret certain of these rituals, in the end the practices of death, mourning and memorialization are remarkably consistent across Jewish communities worldwide.

Judaism and Death

The Jewish concept of death differs substantially from that of its daughter monotheistic religions. One primary difference is the lack of a clear, consistent notion of afterlife. Although there are any number of speculations on ideas of death, life, and existence beyond the phenomenal plane, there is almost nothing in the Torah that deals with ideas of the afterlife or the meaning of death. Interest in these questions grew during the rabbinic period, quite possibly due to the increasing syncretization of multiple philosophies and religious principles among cultures interacting in ancient Israel. There is reasonable discussion of ideas about the afterlife in rabbinic literature, but they do not add up to anything resembling the importance of these questions in Islam and especially Christianity.

The ancient rabbis do discuss concepts of an afterlife where reward and punishment (sekhar v'onesh) are distributed after death based upon one's merit in life. Similarly, particularly meritorious individuals are described as receiving reward in the afterlife. At the same time, traditional Judaism emphasizes one's acts and comportment in *this* life, regardless of consequences after death. An extreme, rather existentialist version of this is a thread that holds an important place on the spectrum of traditional belief: that the essence and central task of Jewish life is the observance of the Torah, that the privilege of doing so is itself the reward, thus obviating the need for a concept of the afterlife in the normal sense. But this concept coexists, even if with tension, with belief in some kind of afterlife as a central theological principle.

In terms of Jewish rituals surrounding death, this theoretical discussion takes a second position to a combination of laws derived from Biblical exegesis and accumulations of folk customs from the rabbinic era through the medieval. For the most part, the Torah's discussion of mourning practices consists of prohibitions against imitating the customs of surrounding people, such as tattooing and cutting the flesh or hair. Thus most laws and customs surrounding death and mourning are rabbinic in origin. They center on two basic sets of obligations: the first is of the family and community to show appropriate respect for the deceased, and the second is of the family to mark time in graduating levels of outward symbolization of grief after death. When a Jewish person dies, and before the body is interred, the closest relatives—which according to Jewish law include parents, children, and siblings—become immediately responsible to attend to the burial (it is traditional to bury, not cremate or otherwise dispose of the body). All other concerns—even observance of positive mitzvot—are suspended, and it is the custom for a funeral to be held as quickly as possible after death. For a deceased person that either has no family or is an unknown person (referred to as a "met mitzvah"), the task of their respectful burial is regarded as a fundamental obligation to the community, the timely completion of which even pushes aside other mitzvot. This requirement, which is honored with intense seriousness, has occasionally caused tension for Jews living in Christian lands, which observe no similar custom. Especially in the early modern period, attempts by outside critics to paint the Jewish community as primitive and inhumane would falsely accuse Jews of risking the lives of individuals by hastily interring those not yet dead in some cases.

Before the funeral, the deceased is prepared in a ritual cleansing, tahara. As we have seen, the primary point of reference for the term "tahara," purification, is the ritual purity of those presenting or offering sacrifices at the Temple. Similarly here, the body itself is cleansed, all dirt, residue, makeup, or any other external adornment is removed. The body is then clothed in a plain white garment, placed (in traditional circles) in a plain casket and is prepared for burial. Modern burial practices, such as embalming, are generally disallowed according to Jewish law. In all traditional Jewish funerals today (which are a considerable proportion of all Jewish funerals), the duty of tahara falls to a special society, the hevra kadisha (literally: holy society). Historically, service in the hevra kadisha was prestigious in the community, its membership was exclusive, and the work considered a solemn honor and obligation. Even today, while the social accoutrements of membership in the hevra kadisha are not the same as they were in the early modern kehilla, its work is considered a duty and privilege of the highest order. Once the deceased has been prepared for burial, if the body is not to be immediately transported for the funeral, it is guarded constantly by volunteer shomrim (guards, frequently yeshiva students), as the body is not to be left unattended from death until internment.

The funeral itself is simple: the deceased is brought to a place of eulogy (in current practice, usually a synagogue or purpose-built funeral chapel). The primary mourners are present, and an article of clothing that they wear, usually a jacket or shirt, is ritually torn in a ceremony called kriah (tearing) to symbolize mourning. This custom is the remaining external symbol of the status of avelut (mourning), which at different times in Jewish history involved other rituals, such as covering the face, putting ashes on the head, among others. In Ashkenazi communities, a representative who may be a clergy member or any informed layperson, intones the rabbinic prayer El Malei Rachamim (God full of mercy), a medieval poem composed in the wake of the massacres of the Crusades that evolved into multiple versions throughout the Ashkenazi world. Once the deceased is transported to the cemetery, additional eulogizing may occur, and then the body is buried. Traditionally, those present physically perform the burial, taking turns filling in the grave.

Once the deceased is buried, the mourners enter a status of avelut (mourning). The mourners are escorted home, where they begin "sitting shiva," a set of practices that is named for the seven days that are observed (sheva meaning seven in Hebrew). Mourners do not bathe, and stay indoors seated on low chairs or cushions. For the length of shiva, it is obligatory for members of the community to visit and comfort the mourners, and prayer services for all prayers (except for Shabbat services) are held in the home of the mourner. This both allows the mourner to sit shiva uninterrupted as well as providing a minyan for one of the most well-known rituals of mourning, recitation of the Kaddish prayer. Mourners are expected to recite Kaddish three times a day for eleven months. Traditionally, this practice is understood as a demonstration of the merits of the deceased in having family and heirs to sanctify God's name in their honor, yet another allusion to an idea of afterlife. In this case, the soul (neshama) of the deceased is understood to be enhanced by the prayers of those left behind. Beyond Kaddish, a number of other observances may be performed for the "aliyat ha-neshama" (ascension of the soul) of the deceased, such as learning a designated amount of Torah or Talmud. After the end of shiva, mourners observe a period called shloshim (thirty), referring again to the thirty days of this observance, during which time the mourner returns to most of their daily life but avoids any celebrations or joyful gatherings, does not shave or cut their hair or wear freshly-laundered clothes. At the conclusion of shloshim, the primary mourning ritual is recitation of Kaddish three times daily for eleven months.

As we have hopefully seen in this chapter, the rhythms, rituals and rites of passage of life in the Jewish community are yet another dimension in the construction of Jewish culture. As with religious practice, these observances are followed by many in their traditional form, in adapted form by many more, and in many cases not observed at all, but in aggregate they give a general picture of Jewish patterns of life. Let us now turn to our final arena of Jewish cultural identity: the nation.

Chapter 3

People, Nation, Diaspora, Israel: The Culture of the Jewish Nation

Of all the expressions of Jewish culture, it is our final model, the Jews as a nation, that is both the most familiar and most controversial to modern eyes. The reason for this is obvious: after nearly 2,000 years of existence as a minority religious group among alien (often hostile) majority societies and cultures, in 1948 the international community assented contentiously in recognizing a modern Jewish nation state, Israel. For many, if not most Jews, this creation of a modern political state was a re-creation: it was a return of the "natural" national identity of the Jewish people that had been shattered by the brutal conquest of the land by the Roman empire. Indeed, to members of the Zionist movement that formed the intellectual and physical vanguard in the creation of Israel, this was precisely the belief. Although neither the creation of the State of Israel (Medinat Yisrael), nor the identification of Jewish history with this Zionist narrative was universally supported by Jews, in short order Israel has became a rallying point of Jewish identity both in Israel and the Diaspora, and to this day remains perhaps its most important pillar.

Israel's creation upended many of the basic assumptions and modes of life of Jews throughout the world. For the largely integrated Jews of the United States (which, after the Holocaust, became the largest Diaspora Jewish community in the world), Israel became, along with memorialization of the Holocaust, one of the two central symbols of American Jewish identity. For the traumatized remnant of European Jews, almost wiped out entirely by the atrocities of the Nazi regime and its associated allies in the Holocaust, Israel was a new home and refuge and served as a central destination for survivors. For Jews in many Islamic countries, the establishment of Israel ended once and for all any pretext of tolerance. Jews were attacked, brutalized, and pressured to leave in retribution for Israel's creation, and most found refuge there. Thus, in the decade surrounding the establishment of the Jewish State, the two societies in which almost all Jews had dwelt since the ancient period—the Islamic Middle East and Christian Europe—largely disappeared as viable, robust Jewish societies. Indeed, many communities that remained in their old centers have languished, and many disappeared altogether, as Jews have left to seek opportunities in one of the two new Jewish centers of gravity, the United States and Israel.

Although Israeli identity, based upon commitment to a modern Jewish nation state, has come to be taken for granted as a core component of Jewish identity, it has a history of its own. It evolved both out of the long-held, religious and cultural identification with Israel and the modern nationalist movement central in its creation, Zionism, as well as a dramatic re-orientation of attitudes towards Jews in the modern period. This transformation resulted in a reorientation of the core constructs of Jewish identity—shifting from an ideal of Jews as a religious, if ethnically-unified, minority whose national aspirations were an extension of theology, into a modern national group.

Am Yisrael, the Israelites, and Ancient Jewish Identity

As discussed, one of the central foundations of Jewish identity from its origins as a religion was based in a religious awakening (in the form of Abraham's, and later Moses', religious charge), its narrative evolved as the family, clan and tribe-based religion that transcended what in modern terms would be regarded as a strictly religious identity. In the

Egyptian exile, the clans subjected to Egyptian slavery are understood by the Torah as a quasi-national group (the Hebrews or Israelites), distinct from the Egyptians amongst whom they lived. The Torah even describes them living in a separate physical community within Egypt, referred to as "Goshen."

Israelite National Identity and Modern Israeli Identity

Over the course of forty years in the Sinai desert, the Torah's text describes the formation of a religious-national group, Am Yisrael (the people Israel), for whom the fruition of their identity as a group required conquering the land promised to Abraham and his sons. The completion of religious identity formation understood by the text, then, cannot be separated from the Israelites moving onto the land, sanctifying it by fulfilling the covenant with their presence, and establishing there for all time its religious center. Thus several different components of what in modern terms might be understood as distinct forms of identity (religious, ethnic, national) combined into the ancient Israelite identity. Ancient Israel thus reflected a norm in the ancient world, where various permutations of ethnicity, religion and political organization combined and recombined, in much the same way that modern Israeli identity reflects norms of national identity in the contemporary world.

The consolidation of political and religious identity in ancient Israel reached its height in the Israelite political structures described throughout the Biblical and ancient periods. It is impossible to know with certainty the lived experience and self-perception of individual Israelites outside of the texts and archeological record, but the Bible presents this evolution as a process of development from disorganized, itinerant mass identified by their membership in tribes based upon their descent from the various sons of Jacob. The Bible understands this development as both linear and pre-ordained. The tribal structure of early Israelite society appears as a precursor to greater and greater centralization, although from an historical and archeological perspective, the reality was likely more complicated.

After the exodus, the Israelite tribes were assigned allotted sections of the land of Canaan (which were actually home to a number of other groups that are identified repeatedly in the Torah: Hittites, Jebusites, Canaanites, Philistines, Midianites, each of whom become the perennial foes of the Israelites), with a divine command to expel the inhabitants, who are regarded as defiling the land by their presence as idolaters in the sacred land. Over the period of the "Judges," essentially local warlords and strongmen (and women, such as Deborah), the Bible reports repeated conflicts with other local groups as well as the vicissitudes of the religious commitments of the judges themselves, which serve as moral instruction as they are tempted to violate the covenant for various reasons. These included political gain, sex, and avarice; perhaps the most familiar is the story of Samson, who was seduced by a Philistine beauty, Delilah, to violate his religious duties and leadership, ultimately ending in his own suicidal sacrifice to atone for his error.

As the Biblical narrative proceeds, Israelite society evolved from the period of Judges into the period of Kings, beginning with the ascension of Saul, the first Israelite king, a revolutionary change in Israelite society. When the prophet Samuel, who lent religious legitimacy to Saul's reign, withdrew his support —and by extension God's—Saul was deposed for David. David became the ideal Israelite king, and his rise created an Israelite kingdom that was the symbol of the political, religious and national greatness of the Jewish people in antiquity. The messianic ideal as imagined during the rabbinic era and beyond consistently identifies with the restoration of David's throne (the eventual messiah is even referred to traditionally as "Moshiach ben David"—the anointed son of David). Following David's reign, his son Solomon succeeded him in overseeing significant expansion of the Israelite kingdom, along with the consolidation of Jerusalem and its Temple, which he constructed as the cultic center of Judaism. In this monarchy the identification of Judaism with its spiritual center in the Temple in Jerusalem was completed, as was the ideal of the Jewish people as a nation (at least in the ancient sense, if not the modern), an identity only fully realized in a political-religious state.

After David's and Solomon's regimes, the Israelite kingdom gradually declined, and over the next centuries political infighting, external threats from competing local, and in the end imperial, powers led to a slow collapse. Ultimately, the Israelites suffered the same fate as any number of smaller, ancient groups. They were displaced politically, then physically with the expansion of the Babylonian Empire, the destruction of the Temple, and the exile of the royal court and a significant amount of the Israelite population to Babylon in the late 500s BCE. The return of the priestly caste and reconstruction of the Temple seventy years later led to an attenuated reinstitution of Israelite sovereignty in some of the former territory of the old kingdom. Over the next several generations, Israelite society functioned as one among many religio-ethnic groups competing for autonomy and sovereignty at the crossroads of far larger and more powerful kingdoms, with limited success.

As the successive Babylonian, Persian, and Alexandrian Empires traversed the Middle East and Levant, the Israelites sought to preserve and expand their autonomy to the extent possible, mainly through negotiation and accommodation of imperial interests. The height of Israelite power and autonomy occurred during the Hasmonean revolt in the second century BCE, when a Hellenized Jewish leader attempted to rigorously impose adaptation of Greek social customs. When this effort crossed over into religious observances, defiling the Temple and its practices, it led to the revolt of a family of kohanim, the Maccabees, who simultaneously inspired a religious awakening. After consolidating power with the cooperation of the Jewish rabbinic establishment (the Sanhedrin, or Great Assembly) that legitimated their rule in the absence of a new prophetically-ordained king, the Hasomeans completed a significant expansion and centralization of their power over the region, substantially expanding the borders of the original Davidic kingdoms.

Within approximately a century, however, the growing strength of the Roman Empire and internal conflicts curtailed Hasmonean sovereignty and power. Rome dismantled the Hasmonean regime altogether with the installation of Herod as king, making the kingdom a Roman client state, which it remained for the short period before the revolt of 70 CE. Efforts at expanding Jewish autonomy under Rome collapsed completely after the revolt, which ended with the destruction of Jerusalem, the Temple, and the first steps towards the exile of the Jewish people from the land. The exile was completed after the next major Jewish uprising, the Bar Kochba revolt of 132-135 CE. With the collapse of Bar Kochba's movement, the Romans completed the process of evicting the Jews from the central places of importance in the Biblical land of Israel. While thriving Jewish communities would grow in the northern regions (the Galilee, Golan, and into Syria and beyond), the presence of a Jewish national center in Jerusalem (although it remained a Jewish religious center), along with any remaining national sovereignty, disappeared until the twentieth century.

Picture 5. Frieze from the Arch of Titus in Rome depicting the Temple vessels (most notably the menorah) in Titus' triumph after the destruction of the Temple in 70 CE, which many mark as the end of Jewish sovereignty in its own commonwealth.

Diaspora in Two Worlds: Jewish Life among Christians and Muslims

In the aftermath of the expulsion of the Jews of Roman Palestine, Jewish communities began to disperse throughout the Mediterranean, Middle East and Europe. Given the expanse of the subsequent

Diaspora Jewish world, it is hazardous to generalize too broadly. But as a minority religious group living primarily among two monotheistic host societies (Christian Europe and Islamic North Africa, Levant and Middle East), who consistently were pushed into specific economic niches in each and who were forced to negotiate their robust religious identity in the face of the frequent hostility of each society, Jews across the Diaspora shared certain common traits in their communal evolution. One of the most powerful determinants of this negotiation was the view held by Jews of the host societies, which for the most part evolved out of the attitude of these societies' religion towards their Jewish minority (or religious minorities in general).

As for the attitudes of Jews towards their own history, an important cornerstone of belief became the principle that the exile was a temporary, if lengthy, punishment for their transgressions as a people, and would ultimately end. In other words, Jews had a vested religious interest in keeping alive their identity as a unique nation, for it had become an article of belief that, one way or another, Jews would return to the land of Israel and re-establish, either through mundane or miraculous means, the Davidic kingdom and usher in a period of universal peace and unity.

In the Islamic Middle East, Levant, North Africa and Spain (before 1492), Jewish status was governed by the early Muslim concept of "dhimmi." Born out of the early history of Islam and the encounters of Mohammad with Jews and Christians as Islam expanded, and explicitly in the "Pact of Umar," Islam defines those groups who share an intellectual history with Islam—Judaism and Christianity—as having a status different from other non-Muslims. Unlike other religious groups, Jews and Christians are regarded as "people of the book," as groups who revere the same monotheistic deity as Muslims, but who have rejected the succession of the Bible by the Koran and Mohammad's mission. They are allowed to practice their religions in muted form, but are required to submit to markers of their inferior status. The most important of these is the *jizya* tax, mandated by the Koran, to be paid in exchange for the tolerance and protection of Muslims. Other restrictions regarding obligatory clothing or other markers, restrictions regarding occupations, building restrictions, and other largely symbolic degradations were applied at various times, by various regimes, for various reasons. By and large, however, the religious sanction of Jewish and Christian minority status in the Islamic world resulted in a fairly stable and peaceful, often robustly successful Jewish communal life in these regimes.

As a large proportion of the Islamic world (and the majority of Islamic territory where Jews dwelt) came under the authority of the Ottoman Empire in the early modern period, the social and cultural association of Jews' past dhimmi status held significant sway in Jewish life until the twentieth century. While during some periods in different areas religious revivalism or political intrigue might place them in a precarious position of insecurity, for the most part Jews in the Islamic world experienced long stretches of cultural and economic stability and intellectual creativity. Some cities in the Ottoman empire, such as Salonika, became major centers of Jewish economic and communal growth; others, such as the four "Holy Cities" of Ottoman Palestine (Jerusalem, Hebron, Safed and Tiberias), became important locations of religious thought and textual innovation.

By the nineteenth and twentieth centuries, the situation of Jews in Islamic territories became more and more intimately tied to European attempts at exploiting the Ottoman Empire's weakness and expanding influence in the Middle East and North Africa. While Jews benefited from this dynamic in terms of their practical status, most notably in the revision of dhimmi category in favor of creating equal status under law for all Ottoman subjects regardless of religion, overall the modernization of Ottoman territories created new fault lines of conflict over identity and inter-religious relations. By the turn of the twentieth century, Jews of the Ottoman Empire held a variety of attitudes and relationships towards the modernizing state. For most, legal change in status had little impact on their daily lives or their interaction with their non-Jewish neighbors. In some cases,

Jews sought involvement with various modernizing movements within the Empire and embraced their identity as Ottoman subjects and players in the evolving political structure. Finally, many Jews began to identify with a more cosmopolitan, European identity thanks to the network of French-language, Alliance Israelite Universelle schools which appeared throughout North Africa and the Ottoman Empire beginning in the mid-nineteenth century.

Internally, Jewish communities had a great deal of autonomy over their affairs and religious practices. Aside from payment of the jizya and adhering to whatever other symbolic disadvantages they faced as a dhimmi people, Jewish communities in the Ottoman Empire and other Islamic states were expected to govern their own communities and internal issues. For Jews, the primary institution of self-government was the kehilla, a combination of lay and clerical leadership which used halakha as a functional tool for settlement of matters beyond strictly ritual, including financial law, torts, damages, and even issues that would be regarded as issues of criminal law in a secular system. Internal communal culture, reflecting the dress and general social mores in a deeply conservative surrounding religious culture, was both deeply woven in with surrounding Muslim and Christian communities while at the same time developed its own specific niches of economic and cultural life. The dominant cultural influence in Islamic Jewish communities was that of the

Sephardim, Jews who were the descendants of those expelled from Spain in the late fifteenth century and found refuge and demand for their presence in early modern Ottoman expansion.

In Ashkenazi Europe, similar internal patterns of self-governance and autonomy unfolded within a different, more fraught environment. While everyday relations between Jews as a minority group and the surrounding Christian societies varied depending on local factors, an important underpinning of Christian-Jews relations was shaped by Christian theological attitudes towards Jews. As most scholars of Jewish history in medieval Christian Europe agree, the status of Christianity as a "successionist" religion, which viewed itself as the heir to Judaism's core truth but correcting its error and rendering its continued existence unnecessary, played a crucial role in the treatment of Jews in the Christian world. Numerous church fathers, notably Saint Augustine, wrestled theologically with the continued existence of the Jewish people after the rise of Christianity, and what role this paradox played in the unfolding of Christian history. Ultimately, Jews were viewed as a minority whose existence was based upon the premise that they were a perpetual reminder by God of the cost of unbelief in the succession of Judaism by Christianity.

In the early years of Christianity, competition between the still-small Christian movement and various other factions, including Judaism but also older religious practices of Rome, as well as numerous variations of early Christian thought that would eventually become heretical, led to the development of an aggressive, doctrinaire posture towards competing religions. With the enmeshment of Christianity with the Roman state under Constantine in the fourth century CE, the early theological militancy of the Christian church as it became more powerful was an important factor in how it addressed religious minorities, usually seeing them as a threat or competition. So much more was this the case with Judaism, the very continued existence of which was regarded as a rejection of the truths of the Christian message. This was further compounded by the deicide myth, which had its origins in the Christian Bible itself: that Jews had sought the persecution and murder of Christ, thus justifying the persecution of Jews for all time.

Medieval Origins of anti-Semitism

For much of the medieval and early modern period, the dynamic of Jewish-Christian relations on the level of general governance and policy was profoundly affected by a shift in Christian thought and society in the thirteenth century. The church itself, which in Europe had largely consolidated under the leadership of Rome (although farther east, eastern Orthodoxy became more dominant), frequently experienced waves of religious awakening that exacerbated negative attitudes towards Jews, who increasingly were seen as a convenient symbol of spiritual and cultural decline. Persistent social problems, poverty, political instability—even, with the arrival of periodic plague epidemics of the fourteenth century and beyond, health crises—were often blamed on Jews who had, by now in the Christian imagination, taken on almost demonic qualities. Jews were increasingly understood through the irrational eyes of medieval fantasies of conspiracy and witchcraft, and treatment of Jews both individually and as communities suffered accordingly.

Earlier forms of anti-Judaism (all of which, sadly, survived well into the twentieth century) became increasingly violent and connected to bizarre myths such as ritual murder around the twelfth century: that as a necessary part of religious ritual, Jews were required to kidnap innocent Christians (usually children or young women), murder them and exsanguinate them to use their blood to make matzoh on Pesach. Other absurd accusations, such as host desecration (that Jews sought to steal the communion wafer to re-enact the crucifixion in a secret ritual) and well poisoning (that Jews purposely poisoned the wells of Christian communities, leading to the plague), frequently became the pretext for violence against Jewish communities and individuals. This violence often included public show trials, executions and burnings of books and people, as well as periodic expulsions of Jewish populations from Christian cities, towns and villages. Likewise, political and economic maneuvering by competing centers of power in Christian society—between, for instance, the feudal lords and princes who ruled most European territories during the middle ages and local municipal leaders, between both and the church—all used Jewish communities for their own purposes when they could. Jews, frequently caught between competing powers, were often able to play these competing interests to their benefit. Even more often, though, they could be quickly overtaken by a rapid decline in fortune when the balance of power shifted.

In European Jewish communities before the eighteenth century (and in some areas well into the nineteenth), Jewish political power primarily consisted of seeking to accommodate this unstable and frequently hostile environment to preserve the maximum amount of security and safety for the community. For most of the medieval and early modern period, Jewish communities were located in more populous settings, both because of the communal demands of Jewish observance and for the safety of community. Furthermore, as Jewish-Christian relations developed, Jews were concentrated in specific areas of economic life, primarily in occupations that were deemed necessary but religiously or culturally distasteful to the surrounding population. The most well-known of these were the multiple areas of commerce in which Jews were concentrated, especially currency and metal exchange and money lending. Moving into the early modern period, especially in central Europe, Jewish economic life became increasingly precarious due to growing competition in areas that had once been off-limits or of little interest to Christians.

Picture 6. Interior of the Old Synagogue, the oldest synagogue in Krakow, built in the early 15th century.

Inside the community, Jewish life was largely governed by the kehilla. Their settlement patterns usually reflected the legal process by which they were allowed to settle in one place or another, which was almost always a contract of tolerance negotiated between Jewish communal leadership and Christian rulers. Jewish communities were typically granted patents of privilege, detailing the obligations and privileges they were granted as a collective. As

outsiders to the feudal and princely systems which
dictated European politics through the eighteenth
century, the exact nature of their presence in Christian
communities was negotiated—and renegotiated—in
order to establish their exceptional place in society.

Often Jews were able to negotiate considerable
autonomy for their communities in exchange for
their services. By the seventeenth century, it had
become commonplace for jockeying European
powers (again, especially in central and eastern
Europe) to exchange extensive financial support
from wealthy Jewish families or individuals for
infrastructure and (especially) military spending
with guarantees of security and right of settlement
for their communities. These arrangements were
precarious, however, and it was not unheard of for
a prince to default on their debt, confiscate Jewish
wealth and property, and imprison the lender.
Farther east, in what by the sixteenth century had
become a massive, unified territory called the Polish-
Lithuanian Commonwealth, Jews enjoyed a slightly
more advantageous arrangement as leaseholders for
the elite Polish nobility, but the same structure of
privilege in exchange for economic service was the
basis of Jewish communal settlement.

As in the Islamic world, Jews in Christian Europe
in the medieval and early modern periods were
left to a great extent to govern their own internal
affairs. Usually governing powers had little interest
in becoming involved in internal Jewish affairs, save

in periods of intensifying religious fervor, and Jews resisted such interference to the extent they were able. As in the Islamic world, halakha was the foundation of kehilla politics and law. In the Ashkenazi kehilla, a fairly standard system of shared governance developed between the lay leadership (usually the kehillot were oligarchic, and lay leadership posts were generally occupied by the economic elites) and rabbinic leadership. Most moderate to large-sized communities operated multiple synagogues, a mikvah, cemetery, a yeshiva and beyt din (rabbinical court) for social structure and governance—all fell under the administration of the kehilla. In Poland-Lithuania and other areas as well, religious law also dictated economic practice, as Jewish legal principles were used in Jewish courts to adjudicate on conflicts over business practice, monopolies, and the like.

The Movement to Modernity

Starting with the final half of the seventeenth century, after over a century of religious conflict, European rulers began a significant shift in their ideals of statecraft and the roles of the sovereign and subjects. By the late eighteenth century, several key regimes— Frederick the Great's Prussia, Maria Theresa and Joseph II's Austria, and Catherine the Great's Russia— were increasingly influenced by Enlightenment theories of governance. By the end of the eighteenth century, between them these three regimes were home to the overwhelming majority of Ashkenazi Jews, and these "enlightened despots" began to structurally redefine the relationship between the state and the individual. While still autocratic in their attitudes towards rule, they simultaneously eroded older foundations of monarchic authority by using enlightened ideas such as improved education, enhancement of the infrastructure, bureaucracies, culture and economies of their states in the quest for consolidation of their power and expansion of their states.

As the most visible (and, in many cases, only) religious minority, Jews both willingly and unwittingly played an important role in this process. First, a small number of Jews, namely those at the highest end of the economic spectrum, already had significant contact with the culture, and even created relationships with powerful Christian officials themselves responsible for engineering modernization. Their proximity both politically and culturally to elite circles in cities like Berlin, Vienna and Prague resulted in gradual adaptation of the surrounding elite culture's tastes and attitudes.

Secondly, the enlightened despots themselves viewed the integration of Jews into their new visions of a unified, centralized and implicitly more homogenized society as a particularly important task. They viewed the kehilla with more suspicion than favor, and believed it represented an obstacle to more direct control over the Jewish population their state-building projects demanded. At the same time, believing Jews too far out of the cultural mainstream to successfully integrate into the new model, they often relied on the kehillot and its leadership as levers for introducing reforms of Jewish status. By the end of the nineteenth century, though, Jews in most areas of Europe (with the important exception of the Russian Empire) were considered fully equal citizens under the law.

Finally, inside the kehillot, were early figures in a Jewish enlightenment—the Haskalah—whose ideas roughly paralleled the general Enlightenment in its focus on rationalism, education and ethics in a Jewish context. Many of these figures were quick to conclude a confluence of interests between their goals and those of the state. These maskilim (enlighteners) became a small, controversial but important factor in bringing modern attitudes into the still-traditional kehillot. At the same time, they often proved overly rosy in their assessment of the intentions of the government in becoming more actively involved in Jewish affairs. While certainly some strategies of the enlightened despots did have the laudable goal of improving the quality of life of their subjects, including Jews, their attitude towards Jews was based almost entirely on the long history of negative stereotypes and assumptions that characterized Jewish-Christian relations in Europe. The general demand made of Jews was to abandon their traditional practices, communities and ways of life, and enter into the mainstream culture of their host country as much as possible. How much was demanded went from a maximal position (that Jews as Jews could not be loyal citizens, and thus must cease being Jews altogether) to more moderate demands that Jews adapt their religion and life to European sensibilities.

Another important contribution to the decline of the kehilla in Europe came from a counterintuitive direction. This was the emergence of Hasidism, a pietistic and mystical religious revival based on the teachings of a kabbalist and healer, Israel Ba'al Shem Tov (or Besht). While beginning as a small network of mystical conventicles in contact with one another, the ideas of the Besht and his principle follower, Dov Ber the Maggid (preacher), became a dynamic organizing structure for a new form of Jewish communal association. Central to Hasidic theology is the importance of the individual Jew's connection to a charismatic leader, a rebbe or tsaddik (righteous person), who became the new hub of Hasidic communal organization (which continues to this day). The Hasidic movement exploded in popularity between the death of the Besht in 1760 and the first decades of the nineteenth century. It went from a small, regional mystical society to a major social and cultural movement as numerous rebbes, the students of Dov Ber and the students of his students, emerged and established their "courts" (comparisons between the tsaddik and royalty are a common theme in Hasidic thought) throughout eastern Europe. It thus created a competing center of authority and loyalty within Jewish communities. Young men in particular became enthusiastic followers of the movement, and in a short time, Hasidic courts contended mightily with the older kehilla structure. Ironically, once the kehilla had been weakened by government regulation, it was in the Hasidic courts that the most intense and successful opposition to any innovation or modernization emerged. The Hasidic world, which thrives today, learned early in its history to play a different game than the kehilla. No longer concerned with representing the interests of Jews outside their group, they focused their efforts on strategically engaging with the wider world in limited ways to secure their community's isolation and autonomy—which continues to this day.

In the end, it was not enlightenment ideas or religious reaction, Jewish or general, that proved the most powerful force in the rapid change Jews faced over the nineteenth century. Rather it was the larger process of state consolidation, modernization, and ultimately nationalism that had the most dramatic impact. Despite the lengthy and fraught "emancipation debates" that occurred in the late eighteenth century—high-level governmental discussions on the feasibility of Jewish integration into Christian states—in the end, it was the irresistible forces of economics, social and cultural forces in central and western Europe that resulted in the near-disappearance of the Diaspora kehilla as an organizing idea of Jewish collective identity.

With its disappearance, the concept of a unified Jewish nation that transcended the bonds of a religious identity fell to its lowest point. Legal restrictions on Jewish participation in general society fell away in most of Europe. Jews already had made significant strides towards civil equality in western Europe—France had granted full citizenship to Jews as early as 1790, by which time both the Netherlands and England had tolerated, and largely integrated, Sephardic Jews into the general population for over a century. In central Europe, in concert with the re-alignment of Germanic states over the nineteenth century, Jews were granted rights piecemeal, as the state slowly eroded the last vestiges of the kehilla structure. By the 1870s, the entire Jewish population of Europe outside of the Russian Empire were considered full citizens of the countries in which they dwelt. In the growing extension of the Ashkenazi world composed of Jewish immigrants to the United States there were no similar hurdles, as the equality of those of all religious groups before the law was a foundational principle of the country. Even in Russia, retrograde Tsarist policy of discrimination against Jews was increasingly regarded as antithetical to human rights, although these policies would end only with the end of the Romanov regime itself and the establishment of the Soviet Union.

The Birth of Modern Anti-Semitism

In 1890, the parliament of the Austrian Empire passed a law which recognized Judaism as one of the three official religions of the realm (the others were Catholicism and Evangelicalism), and laid out the administrative structure by which it would be governed. This moment of legislative history was one of arrival for European Jews. It symbolized the triumph of an ideal of classical liberalism in central Europe, and specifically the arrival of Jews as full citizens and participants in society, government and culture at every level. Over only a few decades, beginning after the continent-wide revolutions of 1848, Jews had become an essential thread of the larger tapestry of Austrian identity and culture that reached from what is today southeastern Ukraine in the east to Switzerland in the west, and from Germany in the north to the Adriatic. Jews played a key role in most aspects of modernization of the Austrian state, from embracing the education and university system to migrating to the dynamic, and increasingly important, urban centers like Vienna, to serving as the vanguard of the development of modern, white-collar occupations. From the construction of infrastructure that drove Austrian modernization forward, to the financial system which made Austria a serious power of the world economic system, to a contribution to Austrian and world culture through the likes of Sigmund Freud, Franz Kafka, and Gustav

Mahler—Jews took their place as citizens of this new society with great success.

Yet at precisely this moment in European history, the encrusted attitudes and suspicions about Jews as a group inherited from the long history of Christian anti-Judaism evolved into something much more sinister: modern anti-Semitism. As the kind of acculturation in Austria described above appeared to be an accomplished fact, several new social and political factors came into play which would lay the seeds for the worst crisis and tragedy in Diaspora Jewish history, the Holocaust.

One factor in this development was related to the very social changes that had been important to Jewish acculturation: the modernization of the world economy and markets. As such dramatic changes usually do, the trend of modernization favored some, and was devastating to others. In aggregate, Jews tended to experience an improvement in their position through moving into urban areas and into occupations that were well-suited for a modernizing economy. But others, whose financial fortune relied upon the older forms of economic life, were rapidly being displaced by the forces of modernization. A second major component of the new anti-Semitism was a widespread anti-modern conservatism that had become a powerful organizing force in multiple areas of European culture. In harmony with other skeptics and opponents of economic and cultural modernization, these various schools of thought understood the changes wrought by the progress of the nineteenth century—with the considerable improvement of the status of Jews at the top of their list—as accelerating cultural decline and alienation. In art, music and literature, the late metamorphosis of Romanticism turned increasingly towards reification of the mystical and irrational and, in the work of figures such as Richard Wagner, an imagined reconstruction of the ancient past as one of Teutonic domination over inferior "others." This attitude dovetailed with trends in the academy and sciences. Indeed, Wagner himself was an important contributor to this line of thinking in his theorizing in his writings that Jews were constitutionally incapable of artistic creativity, and thus full humanity.

Other expressions of elite anti-Semitism evolved out of new pseudo-scientific ideas about race and society. Based on discredited notions of racial difference and biological determinism, older ideas about Jews—that they were somehow constitutionally different from non-Jews—was thus repurposed from their earlier, religious form. In place of the image of Jews as demonic, secretive and in service of a religion that compelled them to insidiously undermine Christianity, Jews were now regarded as biologically defective, driven by genetic predisposition to attack and destroy those genetically superior to themselves. Often adapting the language of apocalyptic conflict between races and civilizational decline, these theorists understood the social difficulties and cultural conflict of fin de siècle modernity as manufactured by Jews for their own nefarious purposes. The most prevalent was the theory that Jews pulled the strings of a vast conspiracy of world domination, which became the theme of the most famous modern text of anti-Semitism: *Protocols of the Elders of Zion*, a forgery that purported to detail the minutes of a secret meeting of Jewish elders as they plotted to manipulate world events. Finally, in a logical conclusion to the anti-Semitic argument, Jews were regarded by new, more muscular and chauvinistic ideas of national unity as a threat to the survival of the nation. In some cases, Jews were regarded as potential allies and participants in nation building. But for the most part, the new nationalism was increasingly intolerant, nativist and, in many cases, organized around the idea that Jews were anathema to the national project.

Finally, the most dangerous expression of the new anti-Semitism was as a tool of modern mass politics. The moment the idea of anti-Semitism as a political tool came into being was the late 1870s, early in the history of electoral mass politics in central Europe. Although these new governing institutions were just in their infancy, very quickly fault lines emerged as the voice of the common voter was elevated to an engagement in a political process that had not existed before. As was discovered by central European politicians in this era, the ability to manipulate grievances of those who feel displaced by change is a powerful advantage, and by the end of the nineteenth century the first widely successful anti-Semitic political party, the Austrian Christian Social party, became the dominant conservative force in Austrian politics.

But even in countries with a more robust history of open politics and tolerance, such as France and the United States, the rising tide of anti-Semitism and other associated racist ideologies spread to the highest levels of power. In France, this was represented most visibly by the military, a bastion of conservatism and anti-liberalism in a republic with a long history of sharp ideological divides. The fruition of this was, famously, the persecution of Alfred Dreyfus in 1894, a Jewish officer in the central command in Paris, who was falsely accused of passing military secrets to Germany and tried multiple times in a tainted process to clear his name. The Dreyfus trial quickly grew into "L'Affaire Dreyfus," and overt, vitriolic anti-Semitism was revealed as the main motivation of those who believed Dreyfus a traitor in the face of clear exculpatory evidence (including the confession of the actual perpetrator). In the United States, Jews were less the focal point of racial animus. Yet even so, as a major center of racialist and racist ideology, the United States of the Jim Crow era had its own share of anti-Semitic theorists at high levels of government, business and academia. Perhaps most best known was the industrialist Henry Ford, who oversaw and funded an English translation and distribution of the

Protocols of the Elders of Zion.

The beginning of the twentieth century initiated an even more tumultuous period. Trends of alienation and anxiety, the fervor of nationalism and the inability of the weakening nineteenth century states of Europe to balance these conflicting interests, initiated a fatal dynamic. The First World War, a calamity for European states (and no less for their Jewish populations, who, in countries like Russia and Austria, suffered disproportionate atrocities and displacement) both fundamentally transformed the political landscape of Europe and laid the groundwork for further entrenchment of the pernicious ideas that had led to war in the first place.

From a Jewish perspective, the interwar period again demonstrated evidence of a completion of the process of integration and acculturation into European society. Simultaneously, although the conclusion of the "war to end all wars" was supposed to usher in a new phase in human peace and rationality in government relations, the outcome was quite different. A failed peace, punitive reparations heaped upon vanquished Germany, and the fragility of the world economy grotesquely amplified the same pre-war voices that sought to lay the blame for instability and cultural alienation at the feet of the Jews. Between 1919 and the onset of the Second World War in 1939, Jews had achieved equal legal status in every country in Europe and North America. The constitutions of the "successor" states to the collapsed Austrian Empire were all constructed as republics with parliaments and the franchise guaranteed to all citizens. In spite of this, nearly every central-east European country (including Hungary, Romania, Poland, Austria, and most famously Germany) regressed from weak parliamentary systems to autocratic or totalitarian states by the mid-1930s. In each of these countries, the arrival of autocracy was deeply imbued with anti-Semitism and used extra-legal tactics such as boycotts and even violence to counteract Jewish advances. Consistent with modern anti-Semitism since its evolution in the 1870s, these movements uniformly defined themselves by a reactionary posture, and viewed the process of Jewish emancipation and inclusion in civil society as a root cause of economic and social malaise.

Anti-Semitism and Nazism

No European state went so far in the embrace of anti-Semitism as Germany under the Nazi regime, which came to control the German Reichstag in the elections of 1933. Within a shockingly short period of time, the regime and its leader, Adolph Hitler, succeeded in seizing power over all institutions of state, and moved quickly to establish a culture of total control over the German nation. Central to Nazi ideology was the anti-Semitic theorizing of Hitler himself. His intention, laid out explicitly in his writings and speeches, was to reverse entirely the progress of Jewish integration into German culture, and Europe altogether. Coupled with his conviction that it was the destiny of the German people to dominate central and eastern Europe and enslave the "racially inferior" peoples in the service of Germany, the Nazi position all but guaranteed instability and violence.

For Jews in Germany, this began almost immediately with the ascension of the Nazi party. Within a year, laws were enacted that singled out Jews for social and cultural exclusion as well as economic persecution, which would be supplemented repeatedly over the next few years. By the end of the 1930s, a significant proportion of German Jews had fled the country for whatever destination they could, but by this time the collective Euro-American culture of racial ideology had restricted significantly the routes of escape. The United States had passed legislation, the Johnson-Reed Act, which put severe limitations on Jewish immigration to the United States in 1924. Other countries adopted similar immigration restrictions, making the refugee situation of Jews dire even before the hostilities of World War II had begun.

Nazi Germany initiated the war with the invasion of western Poland with Soviet assistance in 1939, and escalated it by invading the Soviet Union itself in the fall of 1940. In the blink of an eye, all of east and central European Jewry, with the exception of those in states allied to Germany, came under direct Nazi military occupation. As the German army advanced rapidly into eastern Poland and the Soviet Union, any pretext at organized concentration or non-lethal displacement of Jews (questionable to begin with) was abandoned, and military units specially organized to "pacify" the occupied regions (Einsatzgruppen) were directly ordered to wipe out full categories of those deemed suspicious elements, which always included Jews. Whereas other categories of political or cultural enemies of the Nazi regime saw discriminate retribution and attack, all Jews were deemed undesirable and subject to immediate execution by these units.

As the war progressed, and the murder of millions of civilians began to take a toll on the psychological and logistical resources of the Nazi regime, in 1942 a secret conference of the Nazi leadership finalized plans to construct fixed places for the mass extermination of Jews and others the regime deemed undesirable. These death camps, most famously the Auschwitz-Birkenau complex near Krakow, Poland, thus became the sites of the continued unprecedented atrocities committed against the Jewish people. Utilizing the infrastructure of railroads and the already-accomplished concentration of Jews in Polish urban centers where they had been confined to poorly-supplied "ghettos," the Nazi regime largely succeeded in the murder of the vast majority of Jews in Europe. Almost no communities were spared. The mass murder was efficient and phlegmatic, its effectiveness aided by the cooperation—sometimes willing, sometimes forced—of the surrounding non-Jewish population, particularly in Poland and Ukraine. As an indicator of the degree of devastation, one need only look at the Jewish population of Poland before and after the war: in 1939, it was estimated at around 2.5 million. In 1945, after the collapse of the Nazi regime, there remained approximately 250,000 survivors. And in the few years of instability following the end of the war, those survivors were increasingly attacked by their Polish neighbors, most famously in a pogrom in Kielce, Poland, in 1946. Today, the Jewish population of Poland is estimated at around 4,000. While in subsequent decades some Jewish communities have attempted to create a critical mass of vitality and population, the results have been for the most part disappointing. Few Jewish communities in Europe (outside of the United Kingdom, France and a few others) can exist as self-sufficient entities, and they mostly rely upon support from the United States and Israel to sustain their institutions.

Zionism, Israel, and Jewish National Identity up to the Present

The devastation of the Jewish population of Europe in the Holocaust was unprecedented in Jewish history. Aside from the physical, psychological and spiritual destruction wrought by the Nazi state and the other collaborating populations (which included significant numbers of non-Germans who were often all too quick to assist in persecution of Jews or to benefit from their dispossession), the end of the war created a massive refugee problem, as the survivors, many of them now stateless, sought some place to rebuild their lives. A number of these refugees were eventually admitted to the United States, Canada, and other destinations in the Americas. The other destination was the ancestral home of the Jewish people, the land of Israel, then in the waning days of the British Mandate.

For six decades leading up to the Second World War, the Jewish population of the land of Israel (first under Ottoman authority; after World War I, under British) had seen a small revolution. Before the 1880s, the yishuv (Jewish population of the land of Israel) was small, extremely poor, and overwhelmingly traditional. It was divided between Sephardim, many of them descendants of refugees from Spain in the late fifteenth century, who were integrated into the dhimmi system; the other population was composed of Ashkenazi Jews, motivated by the religious merit of aliyah (moving to the land of Israel, meaning literally "going up"). Arriving in small waves over various periods in modern history, these Ashkenazi immigrants generally had no occupation (other than the study of Torah) or economic support, and relied on charitable donations (called the halukah) collected in the Diaspora to support those studying Torah in the Holy Land, which is regarded as particularly meritorious.

Picture 7. The Zionist kibbutz of Degania, south of the Sea of Galilee. Degania was among the earliest progressive communes that came to represent the ideals of the Zionist movement and later Israeli identity.

Between 1880 and the 1930s, however, the Jewish character of the yishuv changed dramatically. The reason for this was the emergence of a new form of Jewish national identity, Zionism. The Zionist movement was a young initiative, emerging in the early 1880s and motivated considerably by the acceleration of anti-Jewish violence following the assassination of Russia's Alexander II in late 1881. Its early adherents, mostly young, largely acculturated and educated men and women in central Europe and Russia, became convinced that amplified modern anti-Semitism was no passing phenomenon. They believed it revealed a fundamental truth about existence in the Diaspora: that Jews, regardless of their acculturation or accomplishment in general society, would never be accepted as equals in modern, non-Jewish nations. In one of Zionism's earliest manifestos, *Autoemancipation* by Odessa physician (and witness to anti-Semitic pogroms in 1882) Leo Pinsker, the author starkly opined that the intrinsic nature of nations and nationalism could not integrate the Jewish people. To Pinsker, Jews would never be accepted as equals because their strange existence— neither nation nor non-nation—was anathema to the very nature of the nation. The only solution was for the Jewish people to re-awaken to its own intrinsic nature as a nation, return to its ancient homeland, and establish itself as a "nation among other nations."

Within a short period of time, and especially after conversion to the cause of the charismatic Viennese journalist Theodor Herzl, Zionism went from an obscure collection of poor students, journalists and other enthusiasts to a formal political movement, consolidated in 1897 as the World Zionist Organization under Herzl's leadership. While he did not live long enough to see it, by the beginning of the First World War, the movement became an international effort, drawing the financial and moral support of many thousands of Jews worldwide. Thanks to an early, sophisticated appreciation of the value of work on multiple fronts, the Zionist movement, by 1914, had assisted in the migration of thousands to Ottoman Palestine, as well as in the establishment of basic social, cultural and economic institutions under Zionist control.

The Origins of Zionism

Zionism was a modern nationalist ideology, emerging out of the same crucible of European political and social change as the very nationalisms that were increasingly turning on Jews in Europe. It borrowed extensively from traditional, religious symbols and ideas—especially those, like the redemption of the Israelites from Egypt or the liberation of the Temple under the Maccabees, that served well as ready-made national symbols. But to many of its founders and early theorists, most of whom came to Zionism out of frustration with the durability of anti-Semitism in general European society, it was an identity intended in place of religion. Most early Zionists were, like Herzl, born into highly acculturated families; others, like Herzl's political nemesis Ahad Ha'am, came to Zionism after their disillusionment with traditional Judaism. The early Zionists advocated a robust national Jewish identity, which included knowledge of Jewish history, Jewish texts, and a Jewish language (almost always Hebrew, although a thread of Jewish nationalism would also embrace Yiddish as a national language), but for the most part regarded Judaism itself—that is, the Jewish religion, in any form— as an impediment to this dynamic new identity.

The Zionist movement was small for the first few decades of its existence. It was dwarfed by its opponents, who fell into two categories. The first was the majority of the leadership of the Orthodox world, which (not surprisingly) rejected the premises of Zionism, mostly holding the traditional view that the exile was a divine decree and could only be reversed through God's own miraculous redemption of the Jewish people. To the large number of acculturated Jews in Europe and North America, on the other hand, Zionism seemed a threat to the acceptance they believed they had achieved in European society. Although it is risky to impute the views of leadership as representative of the Jewish attitudes "on the street," Zionism did indeed stimulate a great deal of ambivalence and debate within the Jewish world.

These attitudes changed rapidly in the inter-war period. A powerful symbolic boost to the prospects of Zionism came in 1917, in the midst of the First World War itself. The British government, in one of the many machinations in which all sides in the war engaged to gain an advantage, recognized the post-war ambitions of the Zionists to establish a Jewish homeland in Palestine as part of the territory it intended to control after the collapse of the Ottoman Empire. The Balfour Declaration, as it was named after its author, British foreign secretary Arthur Balfour, while vague and ultimately contradicted by British policy even before the end of the war, was nevertheless a transformative moment in lending support to Zionism, which could now point to a tangible result to its political agitation.

The second major accelerant to shifting worldwide Jewish support to the Zionist cause was, as discussed earlier in the chapter, the general interwar decline of Jewish status in an increasingly intolerant Europe. While the 1920s saw an increase in ideologically-motivated, highly skilled migrants (or olim, as Jewish immigrants to Israel are called) from central Europe that added significantly to the state-building arsenal of Zionism, by the 1930s immigrants were increasingly coming out of desperation, seeking any means to escape the closing trap of European anti-Semitism. While aliyah was not a viable option for most Jews to escape the Holocaust (just as the United States had limited Jewish immigration in the 1920s, Britain began to restrict heavily Jewish migration to Palestine in response to increasing Jewish-Arab conflict), the aftermath of the destruction made it an obvious choice for many survivors. The idea of a Jewish state with its own institutions, own army, and own means of protecting Jewish life could not but be desirable in the aftermath of one of history's most horrific demonstrations of the costs of living as a minority group in a hostile culture. These new olim, whatever their attitude towards Zionism had been before the war, were now highly motivated to secure their own safety in their own land.

Within three years, the combined power of infrastructure laid by Zionist efforts from the earliest days of Zionism, the manpower of an increasingly Jewish population in the region (even in 1948, still dwarfed by the indigenous Palestinian Arab population), and world sympathy for the plight of the Jewish people after the Holocaust led to the world community's support for the creation of a Jewish state as the British Mandate expired. Although created at the same time as other "new" states—such as India—as a product of the geopolitical restructuring that occurred after the Second World War and in the rapid withdrawal of the United Kingdom from its imperial designs immediately afterwards, the State of Israel faced a near-immediate threat to its existence in two forms.

The first of these was the result of a dynamic put into play by the growth of the Zionist yishuv itself and the increasing sense of displacement and threat felt by the indigenous, (then) Ottoman Arab community in the territory in which Zionists hoped to build their new state. As was clearly understood by the leadership of the Zionist movement throughout its history, the Arab population—a complex and multi-faceted society in its own right—presented a moral, physical and political quandary for the Zionist project. As a state-building enterprise that pursued its ambitions in no small part because of anti-Semitic persecution, the reversal of fortune that would inevitably be part of a successful Zionist project presented an irresolvable conflict. The settlers of the "new" yishuv were ideologically motivated, often moved by socialist-inspired optimism towards constructing a new, better, fairer society (many had arrived from the authoritarian Russian Empire), and sought different avenues of engagement with the Arab Palestinian community, but they made few inroads in fostering a common sense of purpose. More characteristic was mutual suspicion, a near-constant quid-pro-quo of seeking to exploit the other for advantage or attack the other for retaliation at a real or perceived wrong. As long as the Palestinian Arab community saw the new arrivals as benign, interaction on various levels—economic, interpersonal, even cultural—happened frequently. When Zionism became an increasing threat, as greater numbers of ideologically-motivated olim (before the 1920s and 30s), and later refugees seeking stability and security (in the 1930s and beyond) arrived, the Arab community became increasingly alarmed, aggressive, and inhospitable to Jewish settlement. This exploded in the aftermath of the United Nations vote.

The second dynamic was geopolitical. By the time of Israeli independence, the consolidating powers in the surrounding, also newly-created nations (the entire region, before the Second World War, had been under colonial administration by Britain and France) became frustrated that their ultimate ambition—total control over the Middle East and Levant by Islamic nation-states (Jordan, Syria, Lebanon and Egypt, all of which were also newly-independent states)—was thwarted by the creation of a Jewish state in their midst. Viewing Israel as a colonial outpost of continued European (later American) domination over the region, these states refused absolutely to grant legitimacy to the new state. As the civil strife between Jews and Palestinian Arabs began to escalate, leading to massive displacement— some of it voluntary, some forced—of Arab Palestinians into surrounding, non-Zionist-controlled areas, the surrounding nations invaded. Although on paper the Israelis were at a staggering disadvantage in terms of numbers, the superior organization, training and motivation (most Jews believed the consequences of an Arab victory would be precisely what the Arab leadership quite willingly asserted: the extermination of all Jews in Palestine) led to victory and even the expansion of what were intended by the United Nations to be the boundaries of the Jewish state.

Over the next couple of decades, the dynamic between Israel and its neighbors did not improve. Egypt, Jordan and Syria rejected out of hand any negotiation or recognition of Israel; Israel, in the meantime, built its infrastructure, collected allies and arms from outside the region, and established an adequate deterrent to invasion and attack. In three different conflicts—the Suez crisis of 1956, the Six Day War of 1967, and the Yom Kippur War of 1973—the resolve of both Israel to survive an onslaught and the ability of its neighbors to back up their genocidal threats was tested. In each instance, Israel prevailed. In 1967, Israel added significantly to its territory to include what is today referred to in the international community as the West Bank (the areas surrounding Jerusalem to the south, north and east—the center of Biblical Israel), the

Golan Heights, Gaza Strip and Sinai Peninsula. Only after their final, catastrophic defeat in a war, launched on Yom Kippur, 1973, intended to strike with the greatest surprise and inflict maximal damage, did Egypt, the most powerful of the surrounding powers, sue for a lasting peace treaty with Israel, which was accomplished in 1978. Jordan concluded its own treaty with Israel, while Syria has never ceased its hostile posture. Lebanon, the small coastal state to the north, has also never achieved a long-term peace; Israel's various attempts over the years to influence Lebanese politics directly or indirectly have neither succeeded in shaping Lebanese policy nor contributed to the state's stability.

Although achieving stability in its relations with two of its neighbors, in the aftermath of the sixties and seventies the status quo of Israeli governance in the territories taken from Jordan, Syria and Egypt has compounded a different problem for Israel: its relationship with the Palestinian-Arab population. The initial end of hostilities in 1948 demanded that Israel find a means to govern a diverse population, as many Palestinian Arabs had remained in place and became a part of the new state's population. Although made citizens of Israel, the Arab population of the new state were subject to martial law for a significant period of the early state. Today twenty percent of the population, with representation in the Knesset, this population nevertheless lives at something of a remove from Jewish Israeli society, and there is substantial mutual ambivalence between Jewish and Arab Israelis. In the areas that Israel captured after 1967, especially the Gaza Strip (a small strip of land on the southern Israeli coast, bordering the Egyptian Sinai) and the West Bank (referring to the west bank of the Jordan river, a sizable territory in Israel's interior, containing a significant length of border with Jordan, centering around Jerusalem), Israel came to govern areas with substantial Arab populations, many of which were made up of refugees from areas within Israel who fled in 1948. Although conquest of this region had been discussed in each conflict faced by Israel since 1948, after 1967 Israel occupied, but left its authority over the area an unresolved question. Since 1967, Israel has struggled with a powerful ambivalence about these territories—or at least one territory: the region referred to by the international community as the West Bank. The conflict over other areas occupied by Israel in the war, namely the Golan Heights and the Gaza Strip, have both been essentially resolved: Israel formally annexed Golan for strategic reasons (the heights, overlooking the northern Jordan Valley, were the regular source of unprovoked artillery and sniper fire from Syria), and while the international community has for the most part not acknowledged this, its claim is not for the most part disputed with much passion. Gaza, an area with lesser national or strategic significance, was ceded to its Palestinian population under Prime Minister Ariel Sharon in 2005. Gaza in particular continues to be a significant problem for Israel, as its radicalized political leadership has waged a continuous campaign of violent harassment which has been repeatedly met with muscular suppression by Israel.

Picture 8. Current map of the State of Israel.

By far the most intractable issue for Israel is the situation in the West Bank. Here, the evidence of Israel's ambivalence towards its expansion in 1967 is the most intense. From a religious perspective, the West Bank, referred to as Yehuda and Shomron (the ancient Israelite names for the region) including the ancient walled city of Jerusalem (which Israel has formally annexed), is the beating heart of Jewish religious, ethnic and national history. From a strategic perspective, withdrawal from a large territory located literally in the middle of the state and ceding it to a potentially hostile foreign government is regarded by many as folly. Thus Israel has pursued a complex policy with regard to what has become the most significant international and domestic issue facing the state. On the one hand, it has encouraged the construction of settlements and outposts, meant to expand the physical presence, and thus strategic control, over what is regarded as a foreign Palestinian Arab population. Over time, this policy has become a powerful motivation for many Jews, particularly those of the dati leumi community (see above), whose synthesis of modern Zionism and Orthodox belief regards the idea of withdrawal from any of the West Bank no less than a blasphemy against divine design. A majority of Israelis who settled in West Bank communities subscribe to this view, although many other non-religious Jews, particularly on Israel's political right, are similarly opposed to recognizing Palestinian sovereignty or ceding Israeli control. At the same time, not wishing to rule over a population that is overwhelmingly hostile to Israel and has a history of supporting spontaneous, murderous violence against Israeli citizens, it has pursued until recently support of an independent Palestinian state in part of the territory. While this "two state solution" has long been a sacred cow in the expected resolution of the Arab-Israeli conflict, and has been accepted for decades as the cornerstone of Israeli-Palestinian negotiations, in the present it is all but moribund, and few predict its revival or success. At the same time, lack of resolution and Israeli concerns over security have created a painful humanitarian reality for many Palestinians, as well as galvanizing much international opinion in criticism of Israel, compounding the complexity of the issue.

Although the geopolitics of Israel is probably the most familiar to the average observer, attention to this single aspect of Israeli society has had a distorting effect on attitudes towards the state. But since its establishment, Israel has successfully created a modern, democratic and pluralistic state. The central institution of government, the Knesset (Hebrew for assembly) is a parliamentary system, and the central governing officer is the prime minister. The state itself is a dynamic economic and innovation powerhouse, its citizens experience generally a higher standard of living, economic, social and political stability than its neighbors. Israel was originally established along lines similar to European Social-

Democratic systems in terms of its civil society and infrastructure, although like most of these countries, in the last several decades has moved in the direction of privatization and more expansive capitalism. Israeli citizens enjoy robust state social services, including education and healthcare. As a state that maintains a standing citizen-army, compulsory service in the army or alternative national service as part of early adulthood is a foundational rite of passage for both Israeli men and women. Most Israelis, although painfully aware of the constant presence of conflict and potential violence, are far more focused on what most first-world states would regard as more mundane matters. A consistent issue of conflict in Israel is actually an internal Jewish issue: relations between religious and secular Israelis. By and large, although the conservative Orthodox (Haredi) community has largely come to terms with its opposition to a secular Jewish state, they exist for the most part as a community apart from the larger body politic. The majority of Haredi youth are not conscripted into the army or other national service due to an agreement made between the founders of the state and the then-religious leadership of the Haredi community exempting youth engaged in full-time Torah learning from conscription. This issue is perhaps one of the most contentious in Israeli civil society, as many non-Haredi Israelis view it, with some justification, as an unjust arrangement.

Modern Israeli Identity

Even in the daily lives of residents of Israel, the perennial tension between forms of Jewish identity is still being played out. As with religion or community, it seems that even a robust national identity, complete in every sense, does not suffice for many to define what it means to be Jewish. And while the tensions in Israeli society, as well as their impact on Jewish lives outside of Israel, often seem as though they are without precedent, in fact so much of what unfolds in Jewish life today is a reflection of dynamics that have been in play as long as the Jewish people itself.

Conclusion: Once again, Jewish Culture, Jewish Identity

So what, then, is Jewish culture?

While we may be no further in finding a definitive answer to this question in this book, hopefully the reader now has a good place to start in understanding just how complex the question is. We come at the end of this survey to the same conclusions with which we began: Jewish culture, the lived expression of Jewish identity in the world both historically and in the contemporary world, has no single foundation or even single origin. Instead, it is an amalgam of many different ideas, historical experiences and attitudes, all played out against the backdrop of dynamic change over an almost unfathomably long period of time, nearly the length of recorded human history, as enacted by a small group which understands itself as deeply embedded in it.

This identity is based in part upon a religious idea: at a moment in human history, the true, unitary God chose to appoint a human emissary, Abraham, to carry an idea of monotheism, ethics and service to this God into the world. Contained in these aspects of the Torah's description of the origins of the ancient Israelite religion is what would eventually become the foundation of Judaism: religious belief, a family or community that is uniquely obliged in carrying forth this belief and living according to its precepts, ideally doing so in the very land promised to Abraham. As we have seen, the narrative of the Torah, and then the rest of the Bible, describes the progress of the Israelites through exile, redemption, consolidation of an ancient commonwealth which passed through multiple forms of self-government, only to be scattered, reconsolidated, and scattered again. In each of these stages, ideas of identity and self, both individual and collective, were reinforced, recombined, and reshaped again and again. Thus, I have chosen these three aspects, present in various permutations for all of Jewish history, as the organizing ideas for this brief study.

What this book has hopefully done is add coherence to a very large, very long, and very confusing picture. To accomplish this, I have adopted a specific voice and viewpoint. I have tried to present the unfolding of each of these elements of Jewish identity from the perspective of how they are seen historically by Jews themselves. Of course the claim that one can do this is a useful fiction. There is no single Jewish viewpoint, just as there is no single point of view in any field of human activity, and especially one so complex in its core beliefs about the self and world. Mine, even though it is informed by academic expertise as a Jewish historian, my lived experience as a practicing

Jew, and my career experience as a professor in a university with a Jewish religious affiliation, is still ultimately constrained by the limitations of my own perspective. Of course I do not claim that my view, or even any of its foundations, is somehow more true or authentic than others, albeit informed by years of study and experience. Although I have tried to provide multiple views where important fault lines of opinion and identity exist within the Jewish world, it would be impossible to fully do justice to the many different attitudes that exist. In those areas where my viewpoint is blinkered or falls short, I hope this book will at least assist in furthering the conversation to even greater levels of understanding.

This perspective has shaped the writing of this book, and hopefully added depth and coherence to it. Most importantly, it informs the basic method I have used: to deeply contextualize, both historically and through observations about current practice across communities, each of these three elements of Jewish identity. My position is that while each can be understood in some way through the tools of history, or archeology, sociology, literature—really almost any of the tools of the modern humanities and social sciences—when removed from their deeper, lived context, any analysis will inevitably give a stunted, less-vital picture.

Because beyond anything else, Jewish culture is very much alive, and very much *lived*. For those who identify with it in any of the myriad ways, each of these elements of identity has meaning that shapes day-to-day life. Whether one is an Orthodox Jew, who centers their daily life significantly around religious observance, or a person with no religious affiliation, but for whom their identity as a Jew shapes their attitude towards society and their place in it, their sense of their personal history, their values in whatever way, all have a stake in these issues. "Two Jews, three opinions," goes the old tongue-in-cheek adage many use with self-effacing pride; how much more so when there are fourteen million Jews in the world, for whom these are fundamental issues of self- and communal understanding?

Finally, it is my hope that in trying to bring some clarity and coherence, even in a limited way, to understanding the experience and lives of those in the Jewish community, it will contribute to greater familiarity to its culture to those both inside and outside it. Today, in 2019, while Jews are in many ways more secure than at any time in their history for the last 2,000 years, the ominous echoes of past nightmares are never far from earshot, and recently have grown louder. Although present in the United States for over 400 years and deeply embedded in the fabric of the country for all that time, Jews in the last year in the United States have experienced the worst incidence of anti-Semitic violence in their history, in the massacre of eleven Jewish worshippers at the Tree of Life synagogue in Pittsburgh by an anti-Semitic gunman. Elsewhere, rightist European populism—

experiencing its most sustained growth since the interwar period—has moved with ease back into the anti-Semitic tropes and accusations that many thought were forever taboo after the Holocaust. Israel, the state formed in large part specifically because of the seemingly endless durability of hatred of the Jewish people, has consistently endured an attitude of ontological doubt towards the validity of its very being since its birth. Although many critics of Israel would (and consistently do) point at areas of Israeli governance and policies that are worthy of critique, one need not look hard to detect a dark subtext of exceptionalism, as though Israel has a higher burden, for reasons never clearly explained, to morally justify defending its existence. No other sovereign country in the world faces the same demand from an internationally-coordinated movement that it cede its very claim to being and the right to defend itself against what any other country would regard, justifiably, as threats to it.

It is my view that the only way forward in all of these areas, to make the world a safer place for all, is through deeper understanding. While seemingly a weak bromide for problems that are, especially at this moment, fraught and frightening, the greatest aid to furthering their entrenchment is closing off the avenues of familiarity and knowledge. In the end, thinking critically with the tools of accurate information, knowledge, and the empathy that comes with knowing about others a little more deeply, is the only means of securing a better future.

Further reading

General Reference

Encyclopedia Judaica, 2nd Edition. Detroit: Macmillan Reference USA, 2007.

Baskin, Judith R., ed. *Cambridge Dictionary of Judaism and Jewish Culture*. New York: Cambridge University Press, 2011.

Hyman, Paula E., and Dalia Ofer, eds. *Jewish Women: A Comprehensive Historical Encyclopedia*. Philadelphia: Jewish Publication Society, 2007

General History

Ettinger, Shmuel, ed. *A History of the Jewish People*. Cambridge: Harvard University Press, 1976

Biale, David, ed. *Cultures of the Jews: A New History*. New York: Schoken Press, 2002

Jewish religious texts

Tanakh: The Holy Scriptures: New JPS Translation, Hebrew and English. Jewish Publication Society, Philadelphia, PA.

The Koren Siddur Shalem, English and Hebrew Edition. Koren Publishers, Jerusalem, 2017 (Orthodox siddur)

Siddur Tehila HaShem, English and Hebrew Edition. Kehot Publication Society, 2003 (Conservative siddur)

Mishkan T'Filah: A Reform Siddur. CCAR Press, 2007 (Reform siddur)

Koren Talmud Bavli (English/Hebrew), Noe Edition. Koren Publishers, Jerusalem.

Bible and Ancient Judaism

Ben-Tor, Amnon, ed. *The Archaeology of Ancient Israel.* Translated by R. Greenberg. New Haven, CT: Yale University Press, 1992

Kugel, James. *How to Read the Bible: A Guide to Scripture, Then and Now.* New York: Free Press, 2008

Zornberg, Aviva. *The Beginnings of Desire: Reflections on Genesis*. New York: Three Leaves Press/Doubleday, 1995

Rabbinic History and Culture:

Holtz, Barry W. *Back to the Sources: Reading the Classic Jewish Texts*. New York: Summit, 1984

Urbach, Ephraim E. *The Sages, Their Concepts and Beliefs*. Translated by Israel Abrahams. Cambridge, MA: Harvard University Press, 1987

Schiffman, Lawrence H. *From Text to Tradition: A History of Second Temple and Rabbinic Judaism*. Hoboken, NJ: Ktav, 1991

Medieval Jewish History and Culture

Mark. *Under Crescent and Cross: The Jews in the Middle Ages*. Princeton: Princeton University Press, 1994

Gerber, Jane. *The Jews of Spain: A History of the Sephardic Experience*. New York: The Free Press, 1992

Chazan, Robert. *The Jews of Medieval Western Christendom*. Cambridge: Cambridge University Press, 2006

Modern Jewish History and Culture

Gartner, Lloyd P. *History of the Jews in Modern Times*. Oxford: Oxford University Press, 2001

Diner, Hasia. *Jews of the United States, 1654-2000*. Berkeley: University of California Press, 2006

Rodrigue, Aron and Ester Benbassa. *Sephardi Jewry: A History of the Judeo-Spanish Community, 14th-20th Century*. Berkeley: University of California Press, 2000

Polansky, Anthony. *History of the Jews of Poland and Russia*. Liverpool, UK: Littman Library of Jewish Civilization, 2010

Biale, David et al. *Hasidism: A New History*. Princeton: Princeton University Press, 2018

Meyer, Michael A., ed. *German-Jewish History in Modern Times*. 4 vols. New York: Columbia University Press, 1996–1998

Anti-Semitism and the Holocaust

Poliakov, Leon. *The History of Anti-Semitism* (2 volumes). Philadelphia: University of Pennsylvania Press, 2003

Friedlander, Saul. *Nazi Germany and the Jews, The Years of Persecution, 1933-39* and *The Years of Extermination, 1939-1945*. New York: Harper Perennial, 2008

Yahil, Leni. *The Holocaust: The Fate of European Jewry, 1932-1945*. Oxford and New York: Oxford University Press, 1990

Zionism and Israel

Morris, Benny. *Righteous Victims: History of the Zionist-Arab Conflict, 1881-2000*. New York: Vintage, 2001

Shapira, Anita. *Israel: A History*. Chicago: Brandeis University Press (University Press of New England), 2014

Reinharz, Jehuda and Anita Shapira. *Essential Papers on Zionism*. New York: New York University Press, 1995

Holidays, Life Cycle Events, Customs and Culture

Marcus, Ivan G. *The Jewish Life Cycle: Rites of Passage from Biblical to Modern Times.* Seattle: University of Washington Press, 2004

Kitov, Eliyahu. *The Book of our Heritage* (Orthodox). New York/Jerusalem: Feldheim Press, 1997

Waskow, Arthur. *Seasons of our Joy: A Modern Guide to Jewish Holidays* (Conservative/Reform). Chapel HIll: University of North Carolina Press, 2012

A Quick Immersion series

For more information visit our web site
www.quickimmersions.com

Made in United States
Troutdale, OR
01/29/2024

17256225R00116